The Christian Salt & Light Company

Discovery House
PUBLISHERS
BOX 3566 · GRAND RAPIDS, MI 49501

PUBLISHING BOOKS THAT FEED
THE SOUL WITH THE WORD OF GOD.

The Christian Salt & Light Company

A Contemporary Study of the Sermon on the Mount

HADDON W. ROBINSON

The Christian Salt & Light Company
Copyright © 1988 by Haddon W. Robinson
Discovery House Publishers is affiliated with Radio Bible Class,
Grand Rapids, Michigan.
ISBN:0-929239-02-4
Unless otherwise indicated, all Scripture quotations are from the
New International Version. Copyright © 1973, 1978, 1984, by the
International Bible Society.
Printed in the United States of America
88 89 90 91 92 / CH / 10 9 8 7 6 5 4 3 2 1

TO CAREY WILLIAM
Perhaps at some future time
you will read these words
and understand why
your parents and grandparents prayed
that you would become
a member of the salt and light company.

CONTENTS

TURNING
UP THE
LIGHTS

LEARNING
ABOUT THE
COMPANY

I have given my life to the study and teaching of homiletics, the preparation and the delivery of sermons. For some that sounds as exciting as watching iron rust.

I have found the study of preaching deeply challenging and satisfying. The great preachers—whether known or unheralded—have always spoken to the needs and issues of their times. What is more, they cared about people caught in the minefields of life. They cared enough to warn them and to guide them. And, when they found men and women wounded by the shrapnel, they preached to comfort them. Above all, they were heard. At times some were despised, a few almost worshipped, others applauded or castigated by the press. But even when they were not heeded, they were heard. Those who served God and their congregations best spoke from the Scriptures to the condition of their people in words that ordinary folks in their audience could understand.

Because of my interest in preachers and preaching, I have studied the sermons of the noted preachers of history— John Chrysostom, Alexander Maclaren, George Whitefield, F. S. Boreham, and Charles Spurgeon, among many others. I have also given special attention to the sermons that Luke recorded in his Acts of the Apostles on the assumption that any theory of preaching that cannot explain why Peter's sermon at Pentecost proved as powerful as the mighty wind and fire is not worth talking about.

For some reason I did not give the same diligence to Jesus' Sermon on the Mount until a few years ago. When I did begin to work with it, a disturbing thing happened. Instead of my studying the sermon, the sermon studied me. The preaching of Jesus jumped out of the pages of Matthew, and, rather than hearing Jesus address His disciples and the Pharisees of the first century, I heard Him speak to the pharisee in me.

For almost a year I taught the Sermon to a group of businessmen who struggled out of bed early in the morning to hear the Sermon again. They bought tapes and listened to each lesson several times and assured me that Jesus' words spoken on a hillside in Israel two thousand years ago still made them nervous today. The executives, media people, and workmen in my group echoed the verdict of James T. Fisher in *A Few Buttons Missing: The Case Book of a Psychiatrist:*

> If you were to take the sum total of all authoritative articles ever written by the most qualified of psychologists and psychiatrists on the subject of mental hygiene, if you were to combine them and refine them and cleave out the excess verbiage, if you were to take the whole of the meat and none of the parsley, and if you were to have these unadulterated bits of pure scientific knowledge concisely expressed by the most capable of living poets, you would have an awkward and incomplete summary of the Sermon on the Mount. And it would suffer immeasurably by comparison.

Because of what these studies did for those businessmen, I felt that it would not be presumptuous of me to put them into print. In doing so I acknowledge my debt to commentators who sat on my desk and guided me with their research. To name a few: Martyn Lloyd-Jones, a great preacher himself, has two volumes of sermons on Jesus' single Sermon on the Mount. Donald Carson served me well with his thoughtful and relevant exposition of Jesus' words. Undoubtedly the most important and most scholarly study of Matthew 5–7 published in the last half century is Robert Guelich's, and I profited greatly from his detailed explanations of the text. William Barclay's comments demonstrated again that scholarship does not have to be stuffy. His explanations and applications help the reader to love God with mind, heart, and soul.

I owe thanks or blame to Robert DeVries, an old friend, for urging me to publish these studies, and I am indebted to Paul Hillman, a new friend, for helping me turn the spoken word into the printed word.

In writing about Jesus' Sermon on the Mount, I have the uneasy feeling that I am shining a flashlight on the sun. I comfort myself in knowing that when preachers have been at their finest, that is all they have ever done.

COMPANY GOALS

After World War I, General Pershing planned a series of victory parades through many European capitals. He needed 27,000 soldiers to march in those parades, and each participant was to possess two qualities. Each soldier was to have an unblemished military record, and second he was to stand, at least, one meter, eighty-six centimeters tall.

Forty American soldiers, guarding an ammunition dump about one hundred miles from Paris, read with interest the notice about Pershing's victory marches. What is more each man in the company met the first qualification. None of them had ever been court-martialed.

The second condition, however, puzzled them. They did not know how high one meter, eighty-six centimeters was. The corporal asked the sergeant, and the sergeant didn't know. Then the corporal said, "Well, Sarge, I know that I'm taller than you are." After that it began. Since nobody in camp knew how tall one meter, eighty-six centimeters was, the soldiers began to compare themselves with one another. They stood back to back like children in a kindergarten until they knew the tallest through the shortest men in the company.

Slim, the tallest, kidded his buddies about taking a look at the girls in the capitals and sending back picture postcards. And Shorty knew that if he marched in the parade, everyone else would, too.

When a captain from headquarters arrived to find out if anybody qualified, the soldiers told him their problem, "We don't know how tall one meter, eighty-six centimeters is." So he translated the meter and centimeters into feet and inches and made a mark on the mess hall wall.

Some of the men looked at that mark and turned away, knowing they could not measure up to it. Others stood up against the wall, but they fell short of the mark by an inch or more. Finally Slim stretched himself as tall as possible, but he fell one-quarter of an inch short. Not one of them came to the six feet, one and one-fifth inches that one meter, eighty-six centimeters represents.

Pershing eventually found qualified men who marched in his victory parades, but the point of the story is that when we have an absolute standard it is futile to measure ourselves against other men and women. We must stand up to the mark.

Some folks interpret the Sermon on the Mount as Christ's mark on the wall. This is what we must measure up to in order to gain acceptance with God. If we determine to work our way to heaven, then the Sermon on the Mount describes how we must live. "If you live up to simply the Ten Commandments," these people say, "you'll do all right with God." This popular interpretation has two fatal flaws.

First, it contradicts the rest of the Bible. The New Testament declares many times over that we are justified because of God's grace; that is, we do not have a right relationship with God because we are well behaved, clever, or religious. So if you decide to get to heaven by keeping the Sermon on the Mount, it's like making up your own exam without consulting the teacher. God doesn't have a do-it-yourself plan for getting to heaven. Second, keeping the Sermon on the Mount to get to heaven is the impossible dream. No one can live the standards set in the Sermon on the Mount. So if you choose it as your mark on the wall, you will have shot yourself in the heart. You will condemn yourself to hell.

Although you may feel you are doing better than some others in keeping the Sermon on the Mount, God doesn't grade on the curve. He will grade you on the basis of an absolute standard. The old spiritual said it well, "God wants one hundred percent and ninety-nine and a half ain't going to do."

But if you choose the Sermon on the Mount as the standard, your mark on the wall, you'll fall short by more than one-half of an inch or so. Even the best of people—Pharisees, religious types, moralists—fall as short as an ant measuring itself against the Empire State Building.

A second interpretation of Christ's teaching in the Sermon on the Mount tries to counteract the error of the first view. This approach asserts that Jesus wanted to convince His hearers that they could not possibly measure up to God's righteousness.

In this understanding of the Sermon, Jesus did more than establish the mark; He told us how impossible the standard is to reach. We should not commit adultery or kill, but also we should not lust or harbor anger. By getting at the heart of the matter, the motives behind our actions, He demonstrated that no one could possibly please God on the basis of human merit.

It is true, of course, that the Sermon on the Mount as a standard condemns us, but why would Jesus spend His time making that point to His disciples—to those who were already believers? Why preach an evangelistic sermon to the choir? If Jesus was addressing insiders and not folks on the outside trying to get into the kingdom, then this second view about setting up an unreachable standard misses the point. The disciples were already part of His kingdom; what would be the purpose of telling them how impossible it is to attain God's righteousness on their own?

The first two views about the Sermon focus on individuals. A third approach applies it to nations. It resembles a political platform for governments to adopt. In this interpretation, Jesus wasn't discussing personal morality or individual ethics. Instead He offered a blueprint for a better world built upon His teachings. In other words, if the nations of the world followed the Sermon on the Mount, then the kingdom of heaven would be established on the earth.

One noted figure who read the Sermon on the Mount this way was Leo Tolstoy. After Tolstoy had a conversion experience, He became enamored with some of the teachings of Jesus, and he was particularly impressed with the Sermon on the Mount.

Tolstoy felt that governments needed to submit to the guidance of Jesus. Courts should stop administering oaths to witnesses because of Christ's teaching about not swearing. Since a line in the Sermon says that we are to resist evil, Tolstoy wanted to do away with police forces and armies. If people did not fight against evil, somehow they would usher in God's kingdom.

Tolstoy tried personally to live according to the concepts in the Sermon on the Mount, but when he attempted to get the Russian government to join his crusade, they hounded and persecuted him. In fact, Russian leaders thought he was evil, and they resisted him.

Even if Tolstoy were partially right, the world would not improve much even if nations decided to adopt the Sermon on the Mount as their constitution. Men and women are depraved—individuals and governments. All of us suffer from curvature of the soul. Setting up higher standards of behavior doesn't mean citizens will behave that way. Every nation has better laws than its people keep.

This change-the-world approach to the Sermon gained popularity in the United States at the turn of the century. The progressive idealism in politics was baptized into the Christian faith uncorrected. Every day and in every way the world was to get better and better. The Sermon on the Mount was a manifesto for great political programs.That philosophy has few supporters today. Two world wars blasted it out of contention, and not many politicians or religious leaders would seriously defend that proposition today. Not only does this view resemble blue sky, but also we should dismiss it because it does not fit the context of the Sermon on the Mount. Jesus was not addressing a first century United Nations meeting; He was not urging political leaders to adopt a new ethic.

A fourth group of interpreters have seen the Sermon on the Mount as a life-style for the disciples who were to enter the kingdom that Jesus was about to set up on the earth. This takes the context somewhat more seriously. Jesus did preach about the kingdom, proclaiming, "Repent for the kingdom of heaven is near" (Matthew 4:17). Adherents of this view assert that the Sermon on the Mount was an instruction manual for the two or three years before this kingdom would be ushered in. When that kingdom was rejected by the Jewish leaders, the Sermon on the Mount was no longer operative until the establishment of a future kingdom. The Sermon becomes the ethic for Christ's followers in the kingdom to come. This view is not without its problems.

Jesus said at the end of the Beatitudes that blessing will come as a result of being persecuted as righteous people. If this happens in the millennium, God's golden age, who are the persecutors? In Matthew 6 Jesus spoke of want and worry. Would these be part of His kingdom? To relegate the Sermon's principles to the sweet by and by as an ethic for how people are to behave in a future ideal age is to miss the Sermon's thrust. Christ's Sermon may make us nervous, but there is little in the context or the Sermon itself that allows us to relegate it to some future time. Matthew wrote his gospel after the death and resurrection of Jesus to the churches in the first century and to Christians who follow in their train.

If we traverse the globe on foot, the first view of the Sermon sees it as an instruction book on how to swim an ocean. The second tells us the swim is impossible; we will drown. The third contends that if people in every nation will take the Sermon seriously we can swim the ocean together. The fourth looks forward to a better day when it will be easier to swim across the ocean than it is now. None of these views charts the right course.

In his book *The Quest for the Historical Jesus,* Albert Schweitzer described the Sermon on the Mount as an interim ethic. Jesus was giving His followers an ethic to follow until His kingdom was established on earth, and this was how they were to behave until that event occurred. Albert Schweitzer may have been on to something. The Sermon details how Christ's disciples were to live from the time He gave it until the time He will return to establish His earthly kingdom. This is the fifth and perhaps the best view.

The Old Testament prophets looked forward to a political kingdom in which the Messiah, God's King, would rule over the earth. Without this background, Matthew and the Sermon on the Mount become difficult to interpret. Jesus came to the Jewish people as recorded in the book of Matthew and declared that He was going to establish His kingdom. Now the Sermon on the Mount was the ethic that His disciples were to follow between the time of His promise of that coming kingdom and its actual establishment on the earth.

The mountain discourse was given to the citizens of a kingdom who, in a sense, were destined to live in exile until their Leader returned to set up His kingdom on the earth. They remain loyal to their King; but since exiles do not have land to call their own, they look forward to the King's return and the establishment of a homeland.

The Sermon then is for all loyal followers of Jesus Christ. It is the manner of conduct He expects from them in a foreign environment as they anticipate the time He will return and set up His kingdom.

The message on the mount is not the standard by which we can and will have a relationship to the King. Neither is it the unreachable line on the wall nor a constitution for nations. Nor is it merely something for the future.

The principles of the Sermon on the Mount, and particularly the Beatitudes, are goals to dominate us now, here on earth. They are not ideals. Ideals are unreachable and often frustrate us because they demand perfection to reach them. Christ didn't set up impossible ideals; He established goals, markers and muscle-builders along the way. We may not be able to swim an ocean, but we can dog-paddle a stream, backstroke a river, or sidestroke a lake. We even can crawl-stroke a sea from island to island. Yet reaching a goal is not the end; it only gives us more strength to swim another stroke.

In understanding the Sermon on the Mount, proponents of views one and three convert goals into realizable ideals for pleasing God and ruling nations. Champions of view two turn goals into impossible ideals; backers of view four change present goals into future ideals. All these advocates of different views miss the point; God is more interested in the process than the pinnacle itself. Going after the goal becomes its own reward.

If we were to ask an Olympic swimmer to describe the ideal swimmer, she might say that the ideal swimmer has perfect motion—breathing in sync with every stroke without wasted energy. The perfect swimmer turns quickly, getting the maximum push at the end of the pool. She would be quick to say that no swimmer could ever reach the ideal in every race. An ideal is helpful, but it doesn't motivate an athlete. A goal, on the other hand, is something toward which a swimmer can strive. At times a goal may seem unattainable, but it is not so far off that an athlete cannot work toward it.

If a child in grade school desired to enter the Olympics, the youngster's goal might be to break a world mark set at the last Olympics. It is out there, something toward which that child is going to work. Now at first that goal may seem like an ideal, especially as the youngster learns to swim and paddles from one end of the pool and back. He or she doesn't come close to the record. Yet as that individual continues to practice through high school and college, the goal has a way of flavoring the swimmer's attitudes and actions—disciplines needed to break that Olympic record. The person does not become a perfect swimmer; that's an ideal. But he or she can achieve Olympic standards; that's an attainable goal.

 The problem with an ideal is that it causes us to give up. We decide to postpone reaching the ideal until we get to a sinless heaven. Reaching the ideal through the sheer act of dying, however, is not what Jesus sets before us.

An ideal is what we will be when God makes us all that we should be. A goal is different; we can work toward it now, and our actions and attitudes are affected in the process.

Now, admittedly, when we first look at a goal, we may regard it as an impossible ideal. Like the goal of weighing 156 if we are 295 pounds. Yet it's there; and because it's there, we work toward it. We allow it to <u>influence our eating</u> and <u>dominate our thinking</u>; the goal affects our conduct.

Jesus was setting goals in the Beatitudes and the whole Sermon on the Mount, not impossible ideals. He wants His disciples to strive toward these goals to master a new kind of life. Although we may initially feel like a fourth-grader splashing in the pool, as we press toward the goals they begin to permeate and change our lives.

NEW EMPLOYEES

When a minister preaches at a church service being broadcast on the radio, he speaks primarily to the people in the pews—some committed, others not. He also has a radio audience. The minister is aware of them, but he speaks primarily to those in front of him. Here and there, he may speak to his radio listeners, particularly, at the end of the sermon.

Jesus was speaking authoritatively to His disciples, but the word *disciples* does not always mean the twelve apostles. It refers to those who are learning, and many people surrounded Jesus to learn. Some were true disciples; others went away after a while. His words were too tough for them.

In addition to the committed and fringe disciples, the crowds gathered around. After the crowds heard His teaching, they were amazed because in contrast to their teachers of law He spoke with authority (Matthew 7:28).

Jesus was primarily talking to His dedicated disciples, but He was aware of those disciples on the spiritual periphery. He also seemed to address the crowds at the end of the sermon when He spoke of narrow and wide gates, trees and their fruit, and wise and foolish builders. So Jesus spoke to three groups: dedicated disciples, uncommitted disciples, and the crowd.

WORDS FROM THE TOP

Before Jesus began His Sermon, He went up on the mountainside and sat down. Christ's sitting down may not strike us as being very important, but in the world of the first century, the teacher's position was important. Jewish rabbis might teach while strolling through the market or standing up; but if they wanted to teach authoritatively, they sat down. For example, when the Pope speaks authoritatively, he speaks *ex cathedra*. That means "out of the chair." He speaks with full authority when he does that.

Seminaries often try to get folks to endow a chair—of theology, of missions, of evangelism. One of our seminary constituents wrote, "You want to endow a chair; you are asking for five hundred thousand dollars; I can get you chairs a lot cheaper than that." Well, it's not the furniture, it's the authority associated with the chair.

What is more, many of the versions say that He opened His mouth and began to speak to them. It seems almost obvious; how do you teach if you don't open your mouth? It is almost redundant. But, again, Jewish writings always describe teachers of authority this way.

Sitting and speaking, Jesus told His followers about the principles of His kingdom.

COMPANY MOTTO

"For I tell you that unless your righteousness surpasses that of the Pharisees and the teachers of the law, you will certainly not enter the kingdom of heaven" (Matthew 5:20).

The Pharisees and the teachers of the law prayed, fasted, tithed, and lived according to the rules; but Jesus was not saying that we have to do better than that. He was saying that their righteousness was external. They thought that religious performance made them acceptable to God.

When we stand before God, we've got to do better than that. God requires an inner righteousness, not an outer righteousness. And so Jesus was really saying in the key verse of the Sermon on the Mount that our righteousness has got to be of a different quality.

Putting it another way, Jesus said who we are is more important than what we do. Righteous acts must come from righteous attitudes. That is what the Sermon on the Mount is all about.

ONE

SEAL OF APPROVAL

The editors of *Psychology Today* once published a questionnaire designed to answer the questions: What is happiness? And how do we obtain it? They invited their readers to respond, and a couple of months later the editors put together an article based on the survey. They discovered that pursuing happiness for many was like pursuing a black cat in a dark room at midnight when one is not even sure that the cat is there. One man, for example, when asked about his happiness said, "I don't know. I filled out the questionnaire. I think I'm happy; please verify." The article also pointed out that there were very few factors

MATTHEW
5

that directly correlated with happiness. For example, whether or not one had much money did not have much to do with happiness.

People on the lower end of the economic scale often felt the pressure of not having money, living a thirty-one-day month on a twenty-one-day check. For them money could solve all problems and bring happiness. As a result, winning the lottery was a favorite dream.

The survey revealed that the rich were not happy either. The bluebird of happiness might land on a large home, a big pool, or a big deck, the things of affluence, but deep inside the rich were still unhappy.

The editors received answers from every part of the country, but geography had nothing to do with happiness. Sexual preference didn't make much difference either. The editors found no correlation between pleasure and happiness. We can understand the finding. Some of us have gone to a concert hall and listened to great and very pleasurable music, yet we went out into the cold night and suddenly felt an emptiness inside.

Many people confuse pleasure and happiness. People take narcotics, sniff cocaine, and put heroin in their veins for the high, the tremendous sense of pleasure. The kick is so great that people want to repeat it. Other folks find pleasure by going to the corner bar or by downing a few in the easy chair. But people caught by drugs or alcohol are not happy.

Igor the poet expressed it when he said, "Pleasure is frail, like a dew drop. While it lasts, it dies." And Robert Burns, the Scottish poet, compared pleasure to snow falling in a river. It is white for a moment, but then it melts forever.

The results of *Psychology Today*'s survey shows that we may afford pleasures and enjoy them, but enjoyment does not necessarily equal happiness.

A cartoon pictured a middle-class husband lecturing to his wife. He was seated on the sofa with a blackboard. He had written an equation on the blackboard: "The mortgage is paid; we're fully insured; the kids are okay; we're healthy; and we have each other. It all equals happiness."

And his wife said, "Walter, would you run through that just one more time?" The bottom line is not necessarily happiness.

Perhaps our denseness about happiness is why Jesus grabs us by the lapels at the beginning of the Sermon on the Mount and repeats the word *blessed* eight times. In our English translation *blessed* may not jump out at us; it sounds a little too religious. That's why some of the modern translations use the word *happy* instead of *blessed.* This is okay if we are using it the way the Bible uses the word *happy.*

Our English word *happy* comes from French and from Middle English and has to do with something that is accidental, something that happens by chance. We say that if perhaps something happens, we will be happy. That's not the way the Greek word *makarios,* which is translated "blessed" or "happy," is used.

In secular Greek the island of Cyprus was called the "makarios" isle, the blest isle. The idea was that those who lived on Cyprus never had to leave its shores in order to have all they needed to be content. They had natural resources and minerals. They had a beautiful place to live with fruit and flowers. The island was self-contained. No one had to search for the needs and wants of life.

Another meaning besides "self-containment" comes out of the Old Testament. God blessed men and women, and they, in turn, blessed God. When God blessed them, He was giving His approval. When they blessed Him, they were approving of Him. If they were blessed by God, they stood approved before Him.

When we are blessed by God, we are, in a sense, self-contained; that is, our happiness does not come from circumstances, by accidents, or through diligent searches. It comes because we stand approved before the Creator of the universe. In some way or another, we will seek approval from someone, but we don't all seek God's favor.

If what matters most to us in life is the approval of our loved ones or the approval of our colleagues, then these Beatitudes are not going to do us any good. They deal with how we can stand approved before God. And in knowing that our Creator approves, we will experience true contentment and joy.

To be blessed means to sense the joy, or happiness, that comes from knowing that we stand approved before God. That's why eight times over Jesus spoke about that kind of blessedness, or happiness, that comes out of approval.

TWO

COMPANY
SPIRIT

The religion of the Pharisees is one that is always with us. People who have grown up in religious families understand the Pharisees' system. After all, decent, moral parents give their children rules of behavior, and they have a system of rewards and punishments. The rewards can be very subtle— a smile or word of praise. The punishment can be parental disapproval or more force- ful applications. But such children know the stan-

MATTHEW 5

dards and rules. What is more, if children are part of a religious family, they do religious things. Parents take them to church; they may start as early as the first week after birth. It is not uncommon to see parents bring a newborn out so that all of the religious folks can see the child. Many children's earliest memories are those of Sunday school, church, and religious activities.

In some traditions children of eight or nine respond to an invitation and walk an aisle. In other traditions, children go through confirmation. When they take their first communion, it is the big time. Children know that parents and relatives approve of such activities. So religious behaviors are spelled out, and a child's self-concept comes from that.

How people feel about themselves is determined to some degree by how other people feel about them. If parents say, "Isn't that wonderful; Johnny accepted Christ when he was four" or "Mary just went through her first communion; she has a lovely first communion dress," a child quickly feels good doing religious things. Going to church gives a child a warm glow. If these children skip church to watch television, they often feel guilty.

One of three things can happen to children growing up in a religious home. First, they may struggle through to faith and values of their own.

My daughter Vicki went off to the University of Texas; and after she graduated, I kiddingly asked her what I got out of her education. I had put her through school, and I wanted to know what happened down there at the university. She surprised me with her answer. She said, "Well, Daddy, I went off to the University of Texas and I had your faith and your values. When I got out of the university, I had my own faith and my own values. They happen to be very much the same, but they are mine."

Second, some children may rebel. They have learned the behaviors and have adopted the practices, and they agree with them to a degree. But when they get into high school or college, they kick the traces.

Many parents can tell the story of children who stopped going to church and became atheists after their first year of college. It may seem that such children have lost their faith, but they may never have developed a faith of their own. What children discover at the university is that God doesn't have any grandchildren.

Sometimes a child's faith is handed down like a grandfather's watch. It may be a family treasure, but it is not the child's own. If he or she rebels, it is not against the faith but against standards and patterns that are not his or her own. Behaviors have been externalized, but never internalized.

Third, some children may live by the standards but not have faith inside. This is practice without faith. They go through all of the religious practices and feel good because mom and dad approve.

These children become faithful church attenders as adults, but they don't understand sin in the biblical sense. They are taken up with Mickey Mouse morals. Religion is the fatal five, the sordid six, or the nasty nine. They have strong convictions about those things they don't do themselves. If a person pushes one of their hot buttons, they will drum him out of the church. Nothing bugs these people more than to find someone enjoying what they condemn.

This is not a diatribe against growing up in a religious family; a religious heritage can be wonderful, particularly in learning the Scriptures. But if it ends in self-righteousness rather than a righteousness through faith, it is a tragedy.

Jesus was bothered by self-righteous people—those who really felt they had it all together religiously. They were the folks who knew the rules. They knew the commandments and what righteousness was, and they could live up to it. The severest words Jesus spoke were against folks like these.

The Pharisees were people with outward standards, and Jesus said our righteousness had to exceed theirs (Matthew 5:20). Now they were deeply religious people, those willing to make themselves miserable for the cause. They fasted on Mondays and Thursdays, denying themselves even necessary food. To make themselves so uncomfortable, they had to be earnest about their religion. They had 250 commands to keep and 365 prohibitions to observe, and they tried to be straight as a ruler.

That system of religion was the prevalent one about which Jesus spoke in the first century. But He wasn't saying unless we have 290 commandments and 500 prohibitions, we can't get into heaven. Upping the ante won't help. No, Jesus was saying that one kind of righteousness came from keeping the rules and another kind came from inside. And inward righteousness was what should characterize kingdom citizens. Jesus was talking about people who have found their own faith—those changed inside.

C. S. Lewis, who came the long way around from atheism to theism to finally trusting Christ, concluded that new Christians think God is going to come in and fix the faucets and putty the windows. Instead He does a whole reconstruction job. He tears the walls down and starts at the foundation to build a new structure.

Many times the toughest people to reach are people who live good lives. They've got a nice foundation, the walls up, and they don't want anyone messing with their lives.

If people have the religion of the Pharisees, it is usually characterized by what they don't do. One community is like this—no smoking, drinking, gambling, or carousing. Crosses and stars of David are everywhere. It is the cemetery. Christ's religion is not about death but life.

Jesus was not playing with rules or starting out with negatives. He was saying that something has to happen deep inside to get God's approval, and that does not come from keeping rules. We may keep rules and religious ceremonies and still have true religion, but that is not what causes it.

A man who has worked with alcoholics for over twenty years has wrestled with why some people abstain from liquor for several years and then one day fall off the wagon, yet others quit and never return to the bottle. He said some people become abstainers; others fall in love with sobriety. Abstainers are always in danger of going back; for them quitting is a matter of reform. For lovers of sobriety it is a matter of the spirit.

The difference between abstaining from drinking and loving sobriety is the same as the difference between being religious and loving God. And that's what Jesus is driving at. He is talking about a religion that is on the inside—a quality of life that comes out of a relationship with Him. So blessedness is getting approval from God by a vital and alive relationship with Jesus Christ.

We may feel uncomfortable when we consider the attitudes that should characterize kingdom citizens. That is why people ultimately crucified Christ. The prostitutes and the pimps did not get Him; it was the religious people. Nothing is more uncomfortable than to discover what we thought was going to pass muster doesn't even get us in the front door.

My wife teaches children piano, and I usually sit in my study listening to them. I am amazed at what she is able to do. I am also astounded at the difference between a person who plays the piano and a musician. Some folks play notes, and they hit the right keys for Chopin's *Fantasy Impromptu;* but they don't really play Chopin. Another kind of musician catches the spirit of Chopin. Something goes on inside the performer; and when he or she plays, people pay money to hear the glorious notes. The pianist has captured the spirit of Chopin.

One does not suggest to the spirited player that he or she forget the notes. Notes matter, but hitting the notes isn't what it means to be a musician. Somehow the musician has to have spirit; without it the notes do very little.

Paraphrasing the words of Jesus, unless our musical ability exceeds that of the good note player, we'll never make it as a musician. And that is what Jesus is after. He's not primarily concerned about the notes; he is concerned about the spirit. The person of spirit is the blessed, the approved man or woman.

THREE

BANKRUPTING THE COMPANY

Candidates for president always promise that the next four years will be better than any past years—not only for a few but for everybody. If we just give them enough time, they will lead us to the golden land of prosperity. And not only that, they will give us world peace, beating swords into plowshares,

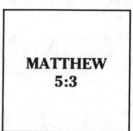

transforming nuclear weapons into farm machines. They will make education number one because they care about the needs of our children. If farmers are having a tough time, a candidate promises if elected to keep prices for grain high. Smart political candidates in the kingdoms of this earth don't campaign by being poor in spirit. That is because they are campaigning in a society that believes leadership, happiness, and success have nothing to do with being poor in spirit.

Blessed and happy people are those who have it all together—the record-shattering athlete, the best-selling author, or the Nobel prize-winning scientist. We don't think of folks like this as poor in spirit.

So when Jesus begins the Sermon on the Mount by proclaiming that the poor in spirit are blessed, He seems to be talking nonsense in our society. It is indeed a paradox. It is like saying, "Blessed are the dependent." Somehow we just don't think that's true.

We can begin to understand what Jesus was saying by explaining what He was not saying. He was not saying, "Blessed are the poor spirited." Wimps of the world and flunkers of personality tests should not unite behind Christ's words. He's not promoting passivity or asking people to imitate Dickens's Uriah Heep, who kept saying, "I'm a 'umble man."

Abraham, Moses, Daniel, and Paul were not poor spirited, uninvolved, letting life happen to them. They could make it through the day without calling their psychiatrist.

Poor in spirit does not mean poor financially either. Slum dwellers merit no special favor with God. That's a myth folks would like to believe, but poor and rich stand equally before God.

Being poor in spirit has to do with our relationship with God. Of the two words for *poor* in the Greek language, the one used here meant absolute poverty. The Greeks distinguished between those who lived hand-to-mouth and those who had nothing at all. The first group lived day-by-day with nothing left over for a rainy day; the second group found every day to be rainy. It wasn't that they didn't have anything left over; it's that they didn't have anything at all.

In essence, Jesus was saying, "Blessed are the beggars in spirit," those spiritually humble. The concept was the opposite of pride and self-righteousness. Yet we have strange ideas about what humility is. We often confuse humility with modesty, and as a result we confuse pride with conceit.

We think humble people have the social grace of modesty. They are the aw-shucks football runners who give all the credit to the line. That may be a nice way to handle touchdowns and life, but these players may not be humble people. The opposite of modesty is conceit, and the opposite of pride is humility.

In the Bible humility is a Godward virtue, and pride a Godward vice. Pride or humility may affect our relationship to others, but the two are most descriptive of who we are before God.

In Luke 18 Jesus told the story of the tax collector and the Pharisee. The Pharisee thanked God that he lived differently than extortionists, adulterers, and tax collectors. He fasted twice a week and gave a tenth of his income to God. What the Pharisee said was true; he was leading an exemplary life.

The Pharisee did not make his living by driving his neighbor to the wall. No contracts with fine print! He shook hands on a deal, and that was it. His word was his bond. And in a day that was as sexually loose as our own, he had not sacrificed his life on a wayside altar. By any conventional standards, ancient or modern, he was a success. He gave a tenth of his net worth every year, not just his income; he was willing to lower his standard of living for God. And his religion had done him good. The people in his community looked up to him. When people of that day wanted a standard of religious success, they turned to the Pharisee.

Apparently throwing reason to the wind, Jesus said the tax collector, not the Pharisee, went down to his house justified. The tax collector was a scoundrel in the ancient world. If we think that he was really a good guy in disguise who admitted his limitations, we don't understand the place of the tax collector in the society of his day. He ranked with the pimps and prostitutes of our time.

In order to make a living, the tax collector bought the right to tax from the Roman government. Because Rome didn't care how much they charged, tax collectors could take in as much as the traffic would bear. Everyone doing business had to stop by the tax collector.

No government publication explained the tax rates. No board of examiners looked over his shoulder, and no one operated without operating with him. We would compare his tactics to those of the Mafia. Anything extra he could squeeze out of them he could keep. Extortion was built into the job. He had hold of the jugular vein, and no one could do anything to get free. He was a traitor to his own people, the Jews, and a pipeline to the Romans.

Tax collectors were the scum of society. When this man prayed, "God, have mercy on me, a sinner," some said to themselves, "He ought to be praying that." If we want a first-rate sinner, we've got one in the tax collector.

When measured by the standards of that society, the Pharisee, without argument, was on top of the heap. Yet Jesus astounded everyone by declaring the tax collector justified. The people then must have said, "That's weird. What's coming off?"

By anyone's standard, the Pharisee was better than the tax collector. Society was better off because he was there. If they both were running for election today, we would be out campaigning for the Pharisee. We would do everything to keep the tax collector out.

And if both of those men wanted the hand of one of our daughters in marriage, we'd be glad to have a Pharisee as a son-in-law—noble, upstanding, good references, a personality that was ten-feet long. But if she dragged that tax collector in, we'd say, "Good night! You can't be that hard up to get married."

What is going on in this story? We would probably say that the Pharisee's problem was conceit. He was certainly the better person, but he should not pray that way in public. We don't stand up and begin a Bible study by saying, "Thank you, I'm here today because I am better than all these other men." It may be true, but we've got to be more modest.

Pious people don't talk like the Pharisee. It just doesn't sit right. He should say, "Aw, shucks, you know, I made the best of what I was."

We think his problem was conceit. We don't like conceit because it is a way of bragging. But that man wasn't put down because of conceit; it was his pride. He was in prayer, in God's presence, and he thought that what mattered in the community mattered in heaven. He assumed God and people were concerned about the same things and that he could pass because he was better than most others in the city.

When Luke introduced the story of the Pharisee and tax collector, he said that Jesus told the story to some who were "confident of their own righteousness and looked down on everybody else" (18:9). One wrong way to decide if we are righteous is to look at other people.

The Pharisee was saying, "Lord, You know that I thank You that I'm not as they are. You made me better, but You had pretty good material to work with. If You didn't have my kind of cloth, You couldn't have made my kind of suit." In the presence of God he thought he was something, but he was nothing. Humility or pride describe who a man or woman is before God. And when we really live before God, we become aware of our tremendous need of humility.

We may dismiss the tax collector's humility. We may say it was easy for him; after all, he had plenty to be humble about. There is some truth to that. That's why Jesus said that it was easier for prostitutes, pimps, and tax collectors than those of wealth, education, and moral standards to enter the kingdom. The former, at least, sense their tremendous need.

Of course, tax collectors can be proud and say, "I thank God I'm not like the Pharisee. I may live a wretched life, but at least I'm open and honest about who I am. I may not pray long prayers and go to church regularly, but I'm not a hypocrite." Some people think hypocrisy is the paramount sin. They could use a short course in guile to cover up the pollution in their lives!

We can make a virtue out of anything if we twist the truth enough, but the point is that the tax collector saw his desperate situation and cried out for God's mercy. That's poverty of spirit, bankruptcy of the soul. It is not how we stand in relationship to other people that matters, it is how we stand before God.

Mt. Everest is approximately five miles above sea level and the Philippine Trench, five miles below. If a diver could look from the lowest spot on earth to the highest, the ten-mile view would be enormously different from what a person can normally see.

But if we could stand on the sun and look at the earth, we would probably say it was as smooth as a billiard ball. With that perspective, we would not see the ten-mile difference between Mt. Everest and the Philippine Trench. The differences that matter on the planet don't matter if we are in outer space.

Some people are Mt. Everest people, and others are as low as the Philippine Trench—great differences from a human viewpoint. But from God's perspective, these differences are inconsequential. It is our sense of bankruptcy that counts.

Two people may each owe ten million dollars. For repayment, one may have one thousand dollars and another, one dollar. One is a thousand times better off than the other; but if they owe ten million dollars, they are both bankrupt.

Jesus was talking about bankruptcy, that deep sense of needing God. If we don't need God, we won't come to Him. And if we don't come to God, we won't be in the kingdom.

It's one thing to write about being poor in spirit; it's another thing to convince someone of its importance. I know, religious people will confess that they are sinners, but they're just being modest. In our society, as a seminary president, I probably pass muster, externally, but the Sermon on the Mount gets me on the inside. I know down inside what I want to be and ought to be, but I know I'm neither.

In his book *Loving God,* Charles Colson noted that when we look at our sins *en masse,* they don't seem to bother us. It is like knowing that we have a national debt of over one trillion dollars; we don't get bothered by that. That's the president's problem.

Somehow we must make our sin more personal. We can worry over owing five thousand dollars much more than we can worry about owing a trillion dollars. When we see individual maggots, we realize how maggoty maggots are.

My mother died when I was a boy, and my dad raised me. He really gave his life for me. One time in college I asked him why he didn't get married again, and my father said, "Well, I wasn't sure that I could marry someone that would care for you as a mother, and I just didn't want to take that chance."

When he got older, he came to live with us. He became senile and began to lose track of time. He'd walk around the house at night and knock on the bedroom doors. He was a child, and I became a parent to him.

One day we were home, and he wanted to go outside. I got him ready; but it was a cold day, and he quickly came back inside. Then he went out and came back in again. After about the third time out and in, I became very irritated. And I said, "Look, either go out or stay in."

He wanted to go out again, but he had no sooner gotten out than he knocked on the door. I was furious. He looked at me a bit confused. He stood there in the door and didn't go either way, so I hauled off and swatted him. I could have punched him in the mouth, knocked him to the ground. When I hit him, he gave me that quizzical look that old people have. At that moment I could have killed him.

It is a horrible memory because of the ugliness inside me that day. With a glimpse like that, I realized the bankruptcy, the depravity of my life. I wish he were still here, but I couldn't honestly tell him that I didn't mean it. I meant it that day. We can excuse my behavior and say, "Old people get that way;

they can be irritating." The truth is, I had a flash—the flash of a murderer.

What happens when we truly see our lives? If we wash it from our minds, we travel alone in our self-righteousness. If we have a sense of bankruptcy, that poverty of spirit, we throw ourselves at His feet and cry out for mercy and forgiveness.

We all need the grace of a forgiving God. Those who understand this make it into the kingdom. As Samuel Rutherford said, "Bow low, man, bow low, the door into the kingdom is low."

Spiritual struggle - engaging, External + internal, Our sense of need for God.

Warren.

FOUR

BAD DEBT

The Arabs have a proverb that says, "All sunshine makes a desert." Yet it is difficult for us to think of sending condolences to a successful business person whose office is perched on the top of the world. The second Beatitude, "Blessed are those who mourn, for they will be comforted," then is as paradoxical as the first and grows out of it. Christ was saying, "Happy are those who are sad." We would like to rewrite this. "Blessed are those who have no tears at all" makes more sense. How can the griefs of life bring the benefits of life? The principle of mourning is not easy to understand. If we mourn about the wrong thing, we are going to be miserable. Some people mourn because they don't have more money, don't have the right job, and don't have as many gifts as some. Others spend their lives mourning about the sick or the dead. None of it helps very much.

MATTHEW 5:4

Growth in life can come when the rain falls, but Jesus was not talking about mourning over unfulfilled dreams or personal tragedies. The mourning here is about grief over sin. In this sense, the second Beatitude is the emotional expression of the first. The poor in spirit are those who sense their need of God and who mourn over their sins.

When we sense our need of Him and mourn about our sins, He comforts us. The Christian life is a cycle of sensing our fallenness, turning to Him, and then standing. The process starts when we realize how far we are from who we ought to be.

I have known some outstanding scholars with first-rate minds. These people are leaders in their field. They got to be leaders because they have a sense of ignorance. People who figure they know it all don't get anywhere.

goal + the ideal

I have a friend who is a leading Old Testament scholar. He said to me several years ago, "I'm fifty-four years of age, and I haven't touched the hem of the garment in my field."

When I was ten, I was constantly reminded of my ignorance by my thirteen-year-old cousin. That is a miserable thing; God should never let that happen! Talk about a bad self-image! My cousin would say to me, "Tell me one thing that you know that I don't know. Tell me! Go ahead and think of something." I knew that I didn't have one card to play. He was three grades ahead of me. Sports, or whatever the subject, he knew more than I. I have learned a great deal since boyhood, and I might be able to keep pace with him now; but at best, we've both only taken on a few more facts.

Sooner or later, we come to a field, whether it be medicine, law, or real estate, where our knowledge runs out. We are then in great shape because that's how we begin to learn.

Sometimes as I sit at my desk, I get very discouraged about what I don't know. The process of mourning about ignorance is not unlike what should be happening in my spiritual life. In sensing my need of God and staying continually aware of it, I draw closer to Him. When I do, I get upset about my sin. The light of His presence shows up the gravy stains in my life. But because I know God forgives my sin, I'm comforted. I know I am a forgiven sinner.

When we're worried about our sin, we don't honor God by thinking bad thoughts about it. We need to go to Him and simply experience His grace and comfort. That is blessedness.

That is why H. G. Stafford wrote:

> My sin—oh, the bliss of this glorious tho't,
> My sin—not in part, but the whole
> Is nailed to the cross and I bear it no more,
> Praise the Lord, praise the Lord, O my soul!

LIGHT

47

Paderewski, the great Polish pianist and composer, had a young woman training with him. She was playing in a recital, and in the middle of her piece, she forgot the music. It sounded as if she was playing bed springs as she hit one wrong note after another. She stumbled through it, but at the end she just sat at the piano and wept. Paderewski went over and kissed her on the cheek. He hugged and comforted her. It wasn't that Paderewski no longer cared about her playing correctly. He knew that comforting the young girl in her failure would motivate her to try again; her frustration was a sign that she sensed her need of more study. And because of his comfort, she wanted more than ever to please him and become a brilliant concert pianist.

Blessed are the poor in spirit, for theirs, and only theirs, is the kingdom of heaven. Blessed are they that mourn, about their sin, about their failure, about their lack of faith, about the way they blow it, because they shall be comforted. And in being comforted they are blessed because they know God accepts them.

Fred Smith told about a couple who took in a messed-up young girl. She lived with them for a year and went through all kinds of problems. Every evening after supper they did something that ultimately made a difference in the girl's life. They had her repeat, "God does not love me because I am good. He loves me because I am precious, and I am precious because Christ died for me."

When that dawns on us—God does not love us because we are good, He loves us because we are precious, and we are precious because He died for us—we will have the poverty of spirit that allows us into the kingdom. Repentance is a recognition of our need. And when we sense that need, we can cast ourselves with reckless abandon at His feet. His grace will meet our need.

FIVE

POWER BASE

While studying for my master's degree at Southern Methodist University, I had a bit part in a university play. The young woman who played the female lead was looking forward to a Broadway career, and she already understood the dog-eat-dog world of theater. Sometimes during the rehearsals we would sit in the blue room 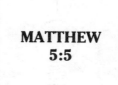 and talk. She had no use for Christianity, less for Christians, and even less for Jesus. She believed only fags and fairies followed Jesus. She couldn't take seriously a man who went around babbling about the meek inheriting the earth. "You and I both know that the meek get ground into the earth," she would say.

MATTHEW 5:5

What that young woman said to me on those occasions was similar to Nietzsche's philosophy. He said that when we look at the ethic of Jesus, bound up in the Beatitudes as part of the Sermon on the Mount, we are listening to the most seductive lie history has ever heard. When Nietzsche came to "Blessed are the meek, for they will inherit the earth," he rephrased it and said, "Assert yourself; it is the arrogant who take over the earth."

We may be for Jesus, but we're not up to defending the idea of the meek inheriting the earth. We're not sure we believe it. In fact, we doubt the idea at both ends. We are not particularly attracted to meekness, and we are uncertain about the meek inheriting the earth. The meek may get to heaven, but we know who gets the earth. The arrogant, the aggressive, the multinational corporations, the Mafia, the porno kings, the military dictators, they're the ones who take over the earth. Successful people claim that we must assert ourselves to get ahead. We must be take-charge people. As Leo Durocher said of Mel Ott and the New York Giants in the 1940s, "Nice guys finish last."

If we handed out placards with the motto "The meek will inherit the earth," few business and political leaders, or religious ones for that matter, would rush to hang them over their desks. Our uneasiness about meekness may spring from its meaning in English. The dictionary defines *meekness* as "deficient in courage," so we think it means to be weak. If we did a word association test, most people would describe a meek man as a Caspar Milquetoast—a person who strains himself in squishing a grape.

The word *meek* in Greek does not mean "meek and mild." Aristotle used the word for the "golden mean." It was the point between extreme anger and extreme angerlessness. A meek person in the Greek sense of the term was controlled and balanced, getting angry at the right things at the right time. Injustice in the world, not personal insults, mattered to this person.

A young soldier in the Peloponnesian Wars wrote to his fiancee about a gift he had for her. It was a white stallion. He described it as "the most magnificent animal I have ever seen. He responds obediently to the slightest command. He allows his master to direct him to his full potential." And then he wrote, "He is a meek horse." The soldier wasn't saying that the horse was shy or even that he was like an old plow horse that allows people to beat him. He was an animal with great spirit, but that spirit was submissive to the rider.

Tied up in the word *meek* is the concept of power under control, the idea of being submissive to someone greater than ourselves. When we look at meekness as weakness, we discover that the examples in the Bible contradict this view, too.

Moses was called the meekest man on earth (Numbers 12:3, KJV). That is a strange description. He started a revolution against the Egyptians and slew one of them in the process. And forty years later when he stood before Pharaoh, the head of Egypt would not have described Moses as meek. This man was not able to lead two and one-half million rebellious people through the wilderness because he was weak, shy, and retiring. In fact, he missed out on the Promised Land because he tried to get water from the rock by smashing it rather than touching it. He doesn't sound weak. How can the Bible describe him as the meekest man of his day? With controlled power and absolute submission to God, Moses was the definition of meekness.

Christ even called Himself "meek and lowly" (Matthew 11:29, KJV). No moneychanger would have called Jesus that; He upended tables and drove the greedy-hearted from the temple.

Meekness is submission, power under control. The Greeks described some winds as meek in contrast to hurricanes, or winds out of control. Perhaps the idea of power under control is best translated by the English word *gentleness.*

We understand "meekness" as "gentleness" better as we see the relationship of the third Beatitude to the first two. In the first one, being poor in spirit means recognizing our personal bankruptcy, our inability to get out of debt to God. It's knowing that deep inside we are sinful people, desperately in need of God's grace and forgiveness. The second Beatitude is the emotional outgrowth of our sense of being poverty-stricken spiritually. As we catch a glimpse of who we really are, we mourn. As we mourn over our individual sins, God comforts us, displaying His grace and forgiveness. Out of our desperate condition should come a spirit of gentleness.

If we think that we are at the center of the universe along with billions of others who think the same thing, the spirit of

gentleness will never be ours. When we believe that everything ought to revolve around us, our views, our wishes, our
businesses, our plans, we will keep bumping into others. If
we live that kind of life, then we will be arrogant and aggressive, always putting people down. We will also put up a front,
afraid to let others know about the unhappiness inside us.
Our masks will be symbols of supposed strength, ways of
hiding our true feelings and making ourselves look superior
to other people.

Henry Drummond was right when he said that anger and
irritation at other people for not giving us "straight A's" in
our lives is probably responsible for more pain than any
other kind of sin. How do we handle the slings and arrows of
others? Jesus said that meekness is a response to who I am
before God; and when we understand who we are, we should
relate to others differently.

Carl Jung, the Swiss psychiatrist, said that we are fortunate that no one ever knows us completely. Of course,
God does; and sometimes in our better moments, we can
catch a glimpse of ourselves as He knows us. But if other
people knew us as we really are, it would be tough, wouldn't
it?

I sometimes get upset when people criticize me. Yet I also
know that if those same people could hear my confessions to
God in the morning, they would know they had not seen the
half of who I am. If they knew what God knows about me,
they would have an ironclad case.

When we live before God and see ourselves as He sees us,
we confess the hidden sins, and that changes our attitudes.
This confession keeps us from being angry and irritated
when people attack us, because we know that if they could
see our hearts, they would have a field day. Out of this
changed attitude comes meekness, a sense of submission, a

gentleness of spirit, and a deep knowledge of what God has forgiven in our lives.

Jesus said that "the meek will inherit the earth." This phrase comes from Psalm 37, where the idea of inheritance is repeated numerous times, and there it refers to inheriting land. It means the same in the Sermon on the Mount. When Jesus instructed His disciples to pray for His kingdom to come, He meant an earthly kingdom, a dwelling place for the meek, those submissive to God. They will not earn it or win it, but they will march triumphantly into it.

Inheritances are given through someone's death, and people simply receive them. When we pray for His kingdom to come, we are not dreaming the impossible. The whole Bible points forward to that day when Christ will return and set up His literal kingdom on earth. And those who are in submission to God, who know their sinfulness, who have admitted it, who have accepted God's forgiveness, to them the kingdom belongs.

But it is also true that the arrogant and the power seekers don't inherit the earth. Hitler followed Napoleon and countless others in his quest for world domination, but God was not on the side with the biggest cannons. Hitler ran into God in the form of a Russian winter and army, and the German people never became masters of the world. Throughout history nations such as Assyria, Babylonia, and Rome have seemed invincible, and if we judged them on a given Tuesday, we might believe it. But if we examine them not by the day but by the years, we discover that the arrogant and the power-mad do not inherit the earth.

What's true with nations is true in the animal world. The lions and tigers should be in control; the lambs should not be baaing anymore. If we were betting people, no doubt we would place our money on the eagle rather than the sparrow. Yet the lion, tiger, and eagle are endangered species. Plenty of sparrows and lambs!

The arrogant and powerful do not inherit the earth. The people in Moscow and Washington don't seem to understand this. They may wipe out a good part of the earth with nuclear weapons, but they will never control it.

The arrogant are not even those who win in personal relationships. No one wants a rude and self-seeking friend. Folks who surround such people want something from them; they don't want their friendship. Those hungry for power are lonely people. They think they possess the earth, but the earth possesses them. They always want more, and soon the envy and desire for more is controlling them. In restaurants, they fight over the best table. At airline counters, they become hostile if they can't get a window seat. In the end all they get is ulcers. They are miserable people. No one wants such people as friends.

The kind, the gentle, the gracious, at least enjoy the earth, whatever it is that they have of it. When they see who they are before God, they know anything they receive is of grace. Hell is what they deserve. And knowing that, they keep power under control, living a gentle and meek life, knowing that one day God will give the earth to them.

SIX

COMPANY
MEALS

Frederick Forsyth, the writer of books about international intrigue, says the greatest motivation in the world is hunger. The fourth Beatitude is about hunger. If we only had the first three Beatitudes about being poor in spirit, about being mourners, and about being meek, we could develop a bad self-image! If we ended up with just those three, we'd admit our sinfulness, our inability to grieve over it, and our cover-up of it before others. In the fourth Beatitude, the focus changes from our needs to our desires—to what we hunger and thirst for. Hunger is sacred, whether one speaks of food, pleasure, or power.

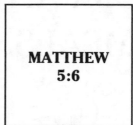

MATTHEW 5:6

Hunger drives us. Advertisers understand this; they know hunger moves merchandise. They motivate us to buy the product by playing upon our deepest desires. Subtly they promise what the product doesn't deliver.

Advertisers make us believe that the basic hungers and thirsts of life will be satisfied by junk food and soda pop. The advertisements for Las Vegas, Reno, and Atlantic City promise happy holidays and the deepest desires satisfied. After a few days of feasting from that table, people discover they have been eating large bites of cotton candy. Fun-seekers leave those places more hungry than when they went.

Christ has a different diet; it starts with hungering and thirsting after righteousness. People in the ancient Near East had meat once a week if they were fortunate. Many lived on the edge of starvation. They had a limited diet; they understood gnawings in their bellies. The Near Eastern sun can turn throats to sandpaper. Desert people felt the sweep of the wind and the hot sand in their faces. The people of Christ's time knew hunger and thirst.

When Christ talked about hungering and thirsting, He meant a deep desire to be righteous, which should come from a realization of need; and He pinpointed that need in the first three Beatitudes. Candy-biting and soda-swigging are not what He had in mind.

Yet I'm not sure that righteousness takes top billing on our desire list. Perhaps we're not really sure what righteousness is. If we've grown up in certain types of churches, we often think of righteousness in terms of negatives—rules and regulations that dampen life and its joys. In these churches, to be righteous is not to go to the places that we want to go and to have to go to the places we don't want to go. It's not doing fun things but those that seem like nonsense. It is the essence of the Pharisees' righteousness. It's negative.

If righteousness is negative, we're not sure that we really want it. Our response to righteousness, as we think we understand it, is like what an Anglican scholar wrote in reviewing a book on the moral authority of the church: "There isn't much in this book . . . that makes the reader want to be good."

It was Mark Twain who said, "Having spent considerable time with good people, I can understand why Jesus liked to be with tax collectors and sinners." Righteousness sometimes turns us off. So the question is, What do we mean by righteousness?

We could take off the *ness* in righteousness, but the *righteous* may not be much better to our ears, sounding like self-righteous. If we do some further cutting by removing *eous,* we end up with the word *right.* Righteousness then is the "desire to be right." As some theologians have put it, "It is uprightness because we are down-right." In other words, as we sense our falling short of what we ought and want to be, and what God made us to be, our desires become different.

Chapter Six

As we see our sin and admit it, we desire to be the kind of person God wants us to be. The great thing about Christ's words is that He did not say, "Blessed are those who are righteous." He said, "Blessed are those who hunger and thirst after righteousness."

When we put down our spouse or spout off to a friend, we may at first defend our words; but when we recognize our ungraciousness, we want to be different. We want to be *right-eous,* a straight ruler rather than a crooked stick. It is this desire that will bring satisfaction to our lives, but without wanting it, we will never get it.

As long as we keep defending our behavior by making excuses, such as blaming family genes when we eat five hundred calories and put on three hundred pounds, we can't have Christ's filling. Hungering and thirsting to be right is basic to being filled. We don't kick hunger or thirst with one meal; hungering and thirsting is a sign of being alive. It is an ongoing process. As the Puritans claimed, "The man who feels not his need to be righteous is the man who needs it most desperately."

It is a mark of life, spiritual life, that we have a hunger and thirst for "right-ness." In certain parts of China, when they bury a person, they put some food, usually bread, and some water in the casket. The corpse never says, "Thank-you." If we dug up the corpse a few days after burial, the bread and water would still be there. Corpses never eat bread or drink water unless they do it at the same time they smell the flowers! What marks a corpse is its deadness; hungering, thirsting, and smelling are out the picture. Hunger is a sign of health and life.

If we do not have an appetite for righteousness, that is a red flag. Something is wrong. To see ourselves as God sees us and to recognize how far we have to go are the

So down — doesn't want to be righteous.
To be Kind, giving, fair; affirming.
See how rough I am — Scorpion stinger out.

beginnings of hunger and thirst. God can fill us, but not with one meal.

We have all pulled away from Thanksgiving tables thinking we could never eat again, yet at five o'clock that afternoon we were back in the kitchen. Dining at God's table once will not take care of hungering and thirsting forever. We must have a constant appetite for "right-ness"; and with that consistent desire, God gives continual filling.

As the old hymn says, "Let not conscience make you linger, or of a fitness fondly dream, the only fitness God requires is that you sense your need of Him." When we sense our need, then we are blessed. The question is, How good do we want to be? If we hunger for righteousness, if we thirst for it, God will fill us, and fill us, and fill us again.

An old Scottish woman used to pray, "Oh God, make me as holy as a forgiven sinner can be." It is a good prayer. And those who pray it out of honesty and integrity, out of a sense of need, are the ones who are blessed. The meek, who live in submission and gentleness before God, will inherit the earth; they are God's kind of people. And blessed are those who hunger and thirst to be right before God. That constant, continual desire, will be continually filled.

SEVEN

COMPENSATION PLAN

When John Wesley was a missionary in Georgia, Governor James Oglethorpe had a slave who stole a jug of wine and drank it. Oglethorpe wanted the man beaten, so Wesley went to Oglethorpe and pled for the slave. And the governor said, "I want vengeance. I never forgive." To which John Wesley said, "I hope to God, Sir, you never sin." In Wesley's time, and especially in the ancient world, mercy was often despised. To the Greeks and Romans, mercy was a sign of weakness. They admired justice, courage, and discipline. As one of the Roman philosophers said, "Mercy is a disease of the soul." The ancient view of mercy was reflected in the culture. According to Aristotle, slaves were living tools and thus were treated in a very impersonal way. For no other reason than being tired of his slaves, an owner could send them to the arena as an evening meal for some red-jowled beasts. If a slave grew too old to work, he could be disposed of like a broken hammer or a rusty plow.

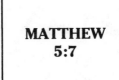

Babies were not treated much better than slaves. If a woman gave birth to a daughter or a crippled son, the father might expose the infant to the elements and allow it to die. And as far as enemies, the only good one was a dead one. It was absolutely unthinkable to have mercy toward an enemy.

In this culture of the ancient world, Jesus proclaimed, "Blessed are the merciful, for they will be shown mercy." We hear His words now and they have a softer sound to us. Mercy may have a good press, but that doesn't mean we are merciful in our culture. We may give some mercy to the underdog, but not to the equal dog or the top dog. We will

Gary Boggs: Football scores - I've been there before.

have mercy on the dependent, but that is sometimes only a way of exercising power. We may have a better regard for mercy because of twenty centuries of Christian influence. But if we look carefully at Christ's words, they may be as unsettling to us as to the people in the first century. Before we can comprehend the fifth Beatitude, we need to understand what the Bible means by mercy.

Evidently the word *mercy* in the New Testament was a Greek translation of a Hebrew word. That Hebrew word is almost untranslatable into English. Perhaps the closest concept is that of sympathy, or empathy. According to William Barclay, the Hebrew word meant to get inside someone else's skin, to look at life from another perspective, to feel what another person was experiencing. But it was more than to feel; it was to act, to think, to will as someone else might in desperate circumstances.

Another way we might look at *mercy* is to compare it to *grace*. Grace and mercy are both reflections of God's love. Theologians say grace is unmerited favor, which means God gives us what we don't deserve. Grace is God's reaction to our sinfulness; mercy is His reaction to our misery.

Several years ago when I was speaking in Oklahoma City, a man there offered to buy me some shoes in appreciation for my ministry. I was a bit hesitant about the whole thing, but he took me to a shoe store and said to the clerk, "I want you to bring out three pairs of brown shoes and three pairs of black shoes. Show us your best shoes and don't let him see the price. He can choose the pair he likes best." Well, it was a good deal and so I responded. That was grace; I didn't deserve the shoes. I wasn't even barefoot!

The man who gave me the shoes didn't show pity on me; I had my own shoes. It was simply an act of kindness. Mercy, in contrast, is a response of grace to people's needs. Mercy is a response to misery; mercy understands the hurt, feels the hurt, and moves out to cure the hurt.

We understand mercy if we have ever had small children. When my daughter Vicki was a toddler, she had a cold—fever, sore throat, stopped-up nose, the whole works. She was miserable and almost too sick to whimper. I picked her up and put her arms around my neck and held her tight. She cried. I got out the humidifier, rubbed her with Vicks, and did everything I could think of. She still couldn't sleep. I stayed up all night with her; I wanted to crawl in that crib and suffer for her.

Biblical mercy, however, is more than showing sympathy for a child. It is feeling for the kid down the street who is suffering because of a broken home but who also has shattered our garage windows three or four times. Mercy has not only the idea of sympathy or empathy but also the concept of thought and action.

In the fifth Beatitude, "Blessed are the merciful, for they will be shown mercy," Jesus set forth a principle of mercy. Some have understood the principle to be "do unto others as you would like others to do unto you, and they will do it." That is, we will receive what we give. The way we behave toward other people will determine how they will behave toward us. This view may be true, but it is only half-true. When we show mercy to others, they are not always merciful in return. Jesus Christ restored a Roman soldier's ear, but that didn't keep the Romans from crucifying Him. It is good to be merciful, but we may discover a number of Romans in society. The merciful are sometimes trampled underfoot.

A second way in which people have understood the fifth Beatitude is that "you should do unto others as you would like God to do unto you." In this case people view the Beatitude from the standpoint of how God will respond rather than how people will respond. And at first glance, that seems like a possibility. However, the Bible never teaches that we can earn God's mercy. God deals with us in grace. God isn't like an investment broker; we don't get grace the old fashioned way, by earning it. It is a gift. God gives it because of who He is, not because of what we do.

If we cannot earn mercy from people or God, what was Jesus saying? He was teaching that "we should do unto others as God in His grace and mercy has done unto us." We can't buy God's mercy; we are the objects of it. In this sense, the fifth Beatitude grows out of the other four. When we see our bankrupt condition in the first Beatitude, grieve over our sins in the second Beatitude, sense our dependence on him in the third Beatitude, hunger because of our desperate need in the fourth Beatitude, He responds in grace and mercy.

The first three Beatitudes deal with our condition; the fourth with our qualification, that is, all we need to be made right with God is the urgent sense that we have a need. If we have been made right with God, what is the evidence of it? The proof that we have obtained mercy is that we show mercy. So mercy does come as a result of mercy. Mercy toward others comes as a result of God's mercy toward us, which is constant and never-ending.

In Matthew 18:21, Peter asked Jesus, "Lord, how many times shall I forgive my brother when he sins against me? Up to seven times?" Peter's problem was that he wanted to know what the limits were on forgiveness. It's easy to take a cheap shot at Peter, but some of us have a tough time showing forgiveness even once.

The ancient rabbis felt that a person should show forgiveness three times. If someone transgressed a fourth time, forgiveness stopped. Peter took the rabbinical standard, doubled it, added one for perfection, and came up with seven times. Who will be a patsy after seven times? Peter's solution seemed quite gracious.

Peter viewed forgiveness like a mathematical formula. One could count it, weigh it, and measure it. It is like responding to the question "How many times should a person love?" with elaborate calculations. To ask such a question is to negate the question.

Jesus responded to Peter's question with the answer of seventy-seven times, or in other textual variations, seventy times seven. Jesus was simply playing on words and saying forgiveness is unlimited. Forgivers are forgetters, and to count to seven, an individual must remember the first six. Forgivers may recollect some incident, but they don't remember it with emotional overtones.

If someone borrowed fifty dollars from you and later paid the debt, you might remember the borrowing and reimbursement of the fifty dollars, but the debt is settled. You would have no emotional overtones in your memory. To forgive and forget doesn't mean that we don't recollect the past, but we're not in emotional bondage to it. According to Jesus, forgiveness must be unlimited; and when we forgive, we don't emotionally drag up the past.

How do we forgive or show mercy the way Jesus taught? Jesus explained through a story. A king wanted to settle accounts with a man who owed him ten thousand talents. This man may have been a tax collector for the king. Whatever he did for the king, it's obvious the man had sticky fingers. A common laborer in those days would have to work twenty years to make one talent. Rome only collected eight hundred talents a year in taxes from the five Jewish regions of Judea, Samaria, Galilee, Perea, and Idumea. This fellow was into the king for ten thousand talents, which might be as high as thirty million dollars in American money.

With this staggering debt, the man was brought to the king. The king ordered all the man's possessions sold and commanded that the man, his wife, and his children be sold into slavery. A slave sold for somewhere between two hundred to a thousand dollars in the ancient world. Under Roman law, debts could be settled this way.

The man begged for mercy from the king and promised to repay him, although he could not do it in a thousand lifetimes. He was like us before God. We recognize the debt we owe God and promise to reform, but we are stalling. The man was buying time, trying to keep himself and his family from being sold into slavery. The king took pity on the man and canceled his debt. He asked for time, but the king gave him a pardon.

The king acted in mercy, and the man left. He soon ran into a companion who owed him about thirty dollars. The man choked him, demanding his money. The small-time debtor pleaded for mercy with the same words that the man had used before the king, but the man had him thrown in prison. It might be possible to repay thirty dollars, but a person can't do it in jail. The man obviously wanted strict justice and revenge more than money. He was going to follow the letter of the Roman law. If a debtor could not pay, he went to jail.

No pity, no mercy. The king dealt with the man mercifully, but the man demanded his rights with others. Word got back to the king about the man's behavior, and the king called him in again. He asked the man a very pointed question, "Shouldn't you have had mercy on your fellow servant just as I had on you?"

Then in anger the king turned the man over to the jailers until he paid back what he owed. At this point, the story concluded with a warning, "This is how my heavenly Father will treat each of you unless you forgive your brother from your heart." These last words were rather dark; Jesus sounds threatening. What does all this mean?

The man in the story heard of forgiveness and accepted it but never entered into it. He took it as a matter of course that the king would forgive him the thirty-million-dollar debt. A sense of being forgiven had never made its way to his inner life.

Christ's parable is a story of us all. We could never pay the debt we owe to God in a thousand lifetimes, and the final warning is to those who have never recognized their poverty of spirit. If they had, they would be forgiving others.

When we enter into God's mercy, we recognize our poverty of spirit, we mourn over our sin, we submit ourselves to Him, and we hunger and thirst for forgiveness. The proof that we have entered into it is that we show mercy to others. The king in the story did not ask the man for gratitude—only the evidence of mercy received in mercy shown.

If we know God's forgiveness, we will forgive. A forgiven person is a forgiving person. If we refuse to forgive, this betrays something about our relationship to God. The fifth Beatitude must be understood in its context. What Jesus is saying in the Sermon on the Mount and throughout the Bible is that the mercy of God and the forgiveness of sins are not theological doctrines to which we give only intellectual assent, they are the experiences of a poverty-stricken spirit, filled with mourning, meekness, and hunger.

Kenyon Scudder, a west coast prison warden, told the story of the small-town Oklahoma boy who had deeply embarrassed his family and community by ending up in prison. While he was in the penitentiary, he heard very little from his folks at home. They were illiterate, so writing was not easy. Yet he wasn't sure whether writing was their problem or if they had simply given up on him. When it came near the time for his release, he wrote his parents that he was coming through their town on the train. The train ran past his parent's backyard, so he told them to tie a white ribbon on the apple tree if they could forgive and accept him. If he did not see a ribbon, he would keep on going and be out of their lives forever. As expected, the man did not get a written response from his parents. He finally left prison and boarded a train for his hometown. As he got closer to the town, he was so overcome with emotion that he moved from his window seat. He had related his story to a nearby passenger and sighed, "I can't bear to look out the window. Will you look for me?" When they came to the town and passed his house, the passenger grabbed his leg and whispered, "The whole tree is white with ribbons."

If we are honest with ourselves, we have all felt like the Oklahoma boy in our relationship to our heavenly Father. I know I have. When I thought of how I had disappointed God, I was afraid to go home. I wanted to send a letter first, asking, "Will you forgive me for all the things I've done?" Finally, out of my desperate need, I journeyed home. Before I even saw my Father, I saw a tree in the shape of a cross. It was filled with white ribbons. Then He rushed out to meet me and hugged me long and hard. He put His arm around me and said, "That's okay, Son, I forgave you a long time ago." When we see the white ribbons hung for us, we hang out white ribbons wherever we go.

why the elaborate reception for the *Prodigal Son*

Having been forgiven much — ask to forgive much.

EIGHT

PURE WORK

Ken Chafin, a Southern Baptist writer, surveyed Baptist seminary students' spirituality with the question, "What does it take to be a good Christian?" He got five different answers. First, a good Christian attends Sunday school and training union. Second, a good Christian goes to the worship services of the church. Third, a good Christian goes to prayer meeting. Fourth, a good Christian tithes and gives to the church. And fifth, a good Christian wins somebody else to Jesus. If you look at those things, at least four of the five have to do with the organization. They have to do with the ritual, with the cere-

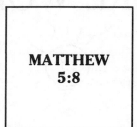

mony. It's not that the ceremony is necessarily wrong, but you could do all of those things and only be a Christian for a week. That's the problem with religion; it sometimes doesn't get to the heart of the matter. People want to see each other; they don't necessarily want to see God.

Christ wants us to see God. He said, "Blessed are the pure in heart, for they will see God." The thought of purity or seeing God is a bit scary. When I was in second grade, just learning addition and subtraction, my older cousin showed me a school paper full of long division. I didn't understand short division, much less long division; but that one glimpse caused me dread for the next year. I confess the sixth Beatitude affects me like my apprehension about long division in the third grade.

I really don't know why the purity Beatitude bothers me, except that it is easy to confuse being pure in heart with being prudish. Sexual purity opponents have done a good job of making chastity defenders seem like fun spoilers—the dull and the drab of the earth. Was Jesus saying, "Blessed are the prudes, for they will see God" or even worse, "Blessed are the sinless, for they will see God"? Down inside I know that if that's what it takes to see God, then I don't have the hope of even a passing glance. If Jesus didn't mean "prudish" or "sinless," what did He mean? We quickly see that the focus of purity is the heart. Jesus was grappling with the kind of purity that comes from deep inside.

The key verse of the whole Sermon on the Mount is Matthew 20:5, in which Jesus declared that our righteousness must exceed that of the Pharisees. Living up to more commands or prohibitions than they had was not His point. The Pharisees had an external righteousness, but Jesus said that we must have an internal religion if we expect to see God. That is the heart of the matter.

In Matthew 15, we read the story of the Pharisees and religious leaders who traveled all the way from Jerusalem to Galilee merely to ask Christ why His disciples didn't wash their hands before meals. They didn't come to discuss hygiene but purification rituals. Just eating could be an elaborate religious ceremony, and the Pharisees had to wash their hands in a certain way. Those religious leaders believed that to see God they had to go through the proper rituals and ceremonies. One Jewish rabbi was arrested by the Romans and only given a couple of bread crusts and a cup of water for a meal. Instead of drinking the water, the rabbi used the water for ritual purification, saying he would rather die than go against the traditions of the fathers. History probably records more deaths for religious traditions than martyrdoms for Christ.

When I was growing up in New York City, some of my Catholic friends went to confession in anticipation of a wild weekend. They confessed not only past sins but also those they planned to commit. They were not taught that in church

I'm sure, and the priest would not have approved of it had he known. My friends made religion external. Catholics do it; Protestants do it, too.

When we base our religion on rituals, we spend a great deal of time evaluating other people's performances. As long as we are outperforming them, we feel good. When we live on that kind of moral ladder, we are always looking at people on the rungs below. We want to feel that we are better than others. And when we do that, we are always looking at other people's sins. We decide which people are the extortioners, the unjust, and the adulterers, especially if none of those descriptions fit us. If we keep taking the measure of people this way, the top measure becomes the lowest measure. Somebody down there is comparing himself or herself to the vilest of people. Adolf Hitler can comfort us because we can say that we are at least better than he. When we constantly compare ourselves with others, God marks us as self-righteous people. Jesus was not talking about ceremonies and rituals but about purity of heart.

When Christ spoke of the heart, He was talking about the core of the personality—the ego, the innermost part of a person. It was not just the emotions. When Tony Bennett sings "I left my heart in San Francisco," he means that he likes the city. He has a warm feeling about it. That is not the way the Bible uses *heart*. The heart includes emotions, but it is more than feelings. It is the totality of our being.

Our emotions come out of the heart (John 14:1), but so do our thoughts (Matthew 15:19). In fact, Jesus said in Matthew 15 that the heart can veil evil thoughts—those of murder, adultery, sexual immorality, theft, false testimony, and slander.

The heart is the seat of our emotions, our thoughts, and our wills. It is in the heart we decide to do good or to sin. So when we say, "Blessed are the pure in heart," we are saying "Blessed are those whose personalities are pure."

What does it mean to be pure? Originally, it meant something clean such as clothing. It was later used to describe grain free of chaff or wine without water. Thus people with pure hearts do not have mixed motives. They are single-minded in their desire to see God.

The first three Beatitudes have to do with our state of being—poor in spirit, mourners over sin, and meek before Him. The poor in spirit recognize their utter need of God. Those who mourn express emotionally what it means to be poor in spirit. In sensing their utter need, they see their sins. Meekness is a submission before God, a recognition of dependence upon Him.

The fourth Beatitude grows out of the first three, for when we see our true condition, we hunger and thirst for God's righteousness, and He fills us. In coming to God and being filled, we are receiving His mercy as the fifth Beatitude indicates. We demonstrate that we have received that mercy by showing mercy to others.

And then in the sixth Beatitude, those who have gone through the hungering, the thirsting, and the filling process exhibit not only mercy but also purity of motive. A pure heart comes from receiving mercy.

But again, the process is a cycle; we are not once and for all pure. That's the way the Beatitudes work. They deliver us from two ditches—self-pity and self-praise. If we had only the first three Beatitudes, we might have a woe-is-me religion. Even if we escape this problem, a puffed-up-chest religion is lurking around the corner. If we follow the Beatitudes all the way, we see that we can't shape ourselves up through moral living or rigid rule-keeping. When we sense our need and are filled by God, we recognize that what happens has nothing to do with our being stalwart individuals, but everything to do with God's being merciful to the weak. Out of God's mercy grows our desire to be pure.

The cycle of our growth continues on and on. We never stop being needy people. Many years into his Christian life, Paul called himself the worst of sinners (1 Timothy 1:15). The more we become aware of our need, the more we become aware of Him; and the more we become aware of Him, the deeper grows our need and longing for His filling, His mercy, His very face. We never need less of Him.

A similar cycle happens in the music world. A youngster just learning piano may play through a Beethoven sonata and come away feeling pretty good about it. But a man like Van Cliburn, who practices ten hours a day, can sight read that sonata and make it seem perfect to the untrained ear. But he goes over it again and again; because the closer he gets to perfection, the greater his distance from perfection. The closer he gets to the goal, the more he realizes how many light years he is away from it.

As we come to know God, we discover that the closer we get to Him, the more aware we become of sin. Out of this awareness comes poverty of spirit, mourning over sin, dependence on Him, and hungering and thirsting for righteousness. As we receive mercy, the more mercy we show, and greater grows our desire to be pure. The purity is not sinless perfection but a cleansing that comes through the process of getting closer to God. As we go through this process, we truly see God.

By seeing God, I mean perceiving, understanding, and sensing the reality of Him. Jesus called the Pharisees blind leaders because they were blind to spiritual things, to God's reality (Matthew 15:14). Moses left Egypt, not fearing Pharaoh, because he saw Him who was invisible (Hebrews 11:27). The burning bush experience had given Moses an awareness and consciousness of God.

We see what we want to see, and who we are determines what we see. Two people go to a museum. One exudes, "That's art!" The other exclaims, "That's art?"

While the pure in heart perceive God, the unpure see other things. When I was a student in seminary, I worked in the post office. At Christmas time, especially, they hired all kinds of extra workers. I can remember being with two men whose hearts were set on sexual immorality. I used to wonder what kind of vermin would indulge in child pornography, but then I worked next to two of them. In all of their jokes and comments, that's all they talked about. Who they were determined what they saw. Perverted sex was all they saw in life.

In this process of becoming pure, we will perceive and see God. We will enter into that reality. We are not sinless, and we are not like Pharisees who are thankful that they are not like other men. The process makes us aware of how much like other people we are, and it produces in us mercy instead of judgment. Although we may be aware of our likenesses with other people, our focus is on God. Instead of looking down the rung, we are looking up at Him. This looking up begins a cleansing process deep down in the heart.

What is our greatest delight? Whom do we delight in most? Bragging about being better than another or satisfying some overwhelming lust are phantoms of delight. Those who delight in the pure are the only ones who will find pure delight.

NINE

PERSONNEL PROBLEM

Washington D.C. is full of peace monuments; we erect them after every war. One cynic remarked that peace is a moment when nations take time to reload. Communists and capitalists use peace as propaganda; pacifists feel they have a corner on it. Yet we are not very good at peacemaking. When Jesus said "Blessed are the peacemakers" in the seventh Beatitude, He was not saying "Blessed are the peace lovers" or "Blessed are the peace eulogizers." We will understand Christ's meaning of peace better when we understand the Hebrew word *shalom. Shalom* is a positive word, not a negative one. When Jewish people say *shalom,* they are not talking about the absence of war; they are wishing all the best for someone.

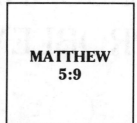

Shalom is an active word, not a passive one. Some kinds of peace are passive. It is not uncommon for two people to fight and settle their argument with guns. Sometimes they end up killing each other. The two dead people have finally come to peace, but it is a very passive peace. A cemetery is filled with peaceful people. Sometimes couples live together in an armed truce, but that is not the peace of shalom. That's more like the detente between North and South Korea; that kind of peace often erupts in trouble.

When Jesus talked about peacemaking, He meant active involvement in bringing together people who were estranged. This is going out of our way to establish peace. The peacemaking Beatitude grows out of the purity Beatitude; people with pure motives want to be peacemakers. People with mixed motives like peace because they don't want to be disturbed, but they are sometimes troublemakers.

The first seven Beatitudes deal with people p
These seven could probably be divided into two
three with the fourth one, the hungering-after-righteousness
Beatitude, in the middle. That is, when God fills His people
with righteousness, the poor in spirit are merciful; the sin-
mourners have pure motives, and the meek become peacemakers. Meek people are particularly suited to make peace.
They are humble of mind and dependent on God. They aren't
arrogant, touchy, or demanding of their rights. Out of meekness can come true peace.

What sort of peace do peacemakers make? One kind is a
peace between God and men. The good news of the gospel is
that we don't have to do anything to make peace with God.
That peace has been already made. God signed a peace
treaty in the blood of His Son, saying that He is no longer
angry. Our sins are forgiven, and all we have to do is sign the
peace treaty. God is satisfied with the death of Jesus Christ
to take away our sin and remove its penalty, and all we have
to do is be satisfied with what satisfies God. God declares
that the cross was enough to end the war. When we agree
with God about that, the war is over.

Peacemakers make every effort to get out the good news
that God is not angry, that peace has been made, and that
the peace treaty has already been signed. At the end of
World War II, the United States signed a peace treaty with
the Japanese; yet in the South Pacific islands, a number of
Japanese soldiers did not get the word. They kept fighting
years after the war ended. In fact, it was only a few years ago
that the last Japanese soldier from World War II may have
been found. For years after the war ended, messengers repeatedly went out to isolated islands to bear the good news
about the peace treaty, but a number of the soldiers shot at
them. They wouldn't believe it, so they kept on fighting.

LIGHT

Isolated in their own selfish ways, many people are fighting God. They won't agree with God that the war is over. Many of them never got the message. One of the kinds of peace that we can make is helping people understand and eventually sign the peace treaty with God.

In addition to peace with God, Jesus may be talking about peace within men and women. As the prophet said, "There is no peace . . . for the wicked" (Isaiah 48:22). Sigmund Freud unscrewed the tops of men's heads and said, "As I've looked into men's lives, I've never met one who is not thoroughly afraid." But no possibility of having peace inside exists without coming to peace with our Maker.

No peace will exist between nations unless peace reigns in each country. And no country will have peace unless peace resides in each community. And no community will have peace unless peace inhabits the church. And no church will have peace unless peace dwells within its people. And no people will have peace unless they surrender to the Prince of Peace.

So peacemakers are helping people find peace with themselves. Many people are walking civil wars because they have never settled the peace issue. If we know the God of peace, we will be people of peace; and this will mark us wherever we go. Instead of driving people apart, we will try to bring them together.

If we can bring people to righteousness, we can establish a communion between them. In fact, we'll find that principle in the Sermon on the Mount. Making peace with a brother is more important than going through religious ceremonies (5:23–24). In other words, we shouldn't bother coming to church if we are bothered with a brother and know we can settle the matter before the service. Peacemaking is of greater consequence than church-playing. Loving our enemies and praying for our persecutors is what peacemaking is all about (5:43–45). That's a tough task. But one way we destroy our enemies is to make them our friends. If we curse them, we put a division between them and us. If we get back at those who get back at us, we are building walls instead of bridges.

Peacemakers drain the moats; they bring people together. In recognition of their work, God gives them new names— sons of God. This is fitting because six separate times in the New Testament our Father is called a God of peace. In every one of Paul's letters, he wrote about the peace of God that comes from the God of peace. If God had stood on His rights and demanded what He deserved, we'd all be in hell. We defamed His name and disobeyed His commands, and He could have demanded His rights. Yet He made the first move; indeed He made all the moves. He sent His Son to make peace through His death. He is a God of peace, so His children as peacemakers are rightfully called sons of God.

The phrase "sons of God" deals with character rather than relationship. When the Bible talks about the children of God, it is dealing with the idea of a father's relationship to a child. But in "sons of God," Christ is denoting a quality of character. Hebrew doesn't have many adjectives, so one of the ways they devised adjectives was to talk about the son of something. Barnabas was called the "son of consolation"; Judas, the "son of perdition." Barnabas was consoling; Judas was doomed. In English when we call someone the "son of a gun," we are talking about the parent. We imply, of course, that the child is as explosive and loud as his mother or father. So if someone is called a "son of God" or a "daughter of God," he or she is displaying God's character.

Whenever we make peace by bringing people into a relationship with God or by bringing two people together, we look a lot like God. It's this family resemblance that marks us out as the sons of God.

Perhaps St. Francis of Assisi's prayer said it best: "Lord, make me an instrument of Your peace. Where there is hatred, let me sow love; where there is injury, pardon; where there is doubt, faith; where there is despair, hope; where there is darkness, light; and where there is sadness, joy." When we live out this prayer, people will call us sons of God. We can do nothing more God-like than to bring peace to those separated from God and from each other.

TEN

OCCUPATIONAL HAZARD

As E. M. Forster noted, "Every now and then people have preferred sorrow to joy." When the first-century Christians signed on, they must have indicated such a preference. Of the eleven disciples left after Judas's defection, ten died vicious and violent deaths. And the one who was spared, John, died a prisoner on the isle of Patmos. The apostle Paul was whipped five times with thirty-nine stripes, beaten with rods, stoned once, and repeatedly hounded and persecuted (2 Corinthians 11:23–27). Early Christians suffered in every avenue of life. We can only imagine what it was like for the Christian stonecutter who turned down the construction contract for a pagan temple. What about the tailor who refused to make garments for pagan priests? What about the couple who declined an invitation from friends to a heathen banquet?

MATTHEW 5:10–12

Christianity split families apart. A wife would come to faith in Jesus Christ, and her husband would be furious. He felt he was put down by others in the city who knew he was a devout pagan. Children were often thrown out of their homes by parents who did not share their faith. Brothers were separated from brothers. This faith designed to bring people together often brought not peace but a sword.

At first glance, the persecution of early Christians doesn't seem to make sense in light of the first seven Beatitudes. Why would anyone want to persecute the poor in spirit? People who see themselves as faded yellow photographs of what they ought to be hardly seem candidates for persecution. And those mourning about their inability to please God don't seem like rabble-rousers.

The meek, those submissive to God, probably don't lord it

over others. In fact, broken-spirited, sin-grieving, dependent people hunger after righteousness rather than for power and fame. They are merciful, pure, and peace-loving people. It just doesn't add up that people with such sterling attributes are beaten to the ground.

Beatitude people should be applauded, not booed. We might expect one of the great hymns of the faith to be, "For he's a jolly good fellow, for he's a jolly good fellow, for he's a jolly good fellow; that nobody can deny." That's why when we come to the eighth Beatitude Jesus again takes us by surprise.

In this last Beatitude, Jesus said, "Blessed are those who are persecuted because of righteousness, for theirs is the kingdom of God." Then He elaborated, "Blessed are you when people insult you, persecute you and falsely say all kinds of evil against you because of me. Rejoice and be glad, because great is your reward in heaven, for in the same way they persecuted the prophets who were before you."

Jesus predicted that the kind of people who demonstrate the virtues of the first seven Beatitudes would be persecuted. He didn't say, "Blessed are you if you are persecuted." We all know religious people who seem to court persecution—those running around with their own stake and box of matches. People want to reject them. They are very zealous people, lapel grabbers with a religion that probably never goes below the shirt pocket. They may think that they bear the offense of the cross, but they are just plain offensive. They've got body odor, bad breath, and bad manners.

Jesus spoke about people being persecuted because of righteousness, not self-righteousness. People may be reviled and punished without being persecuted. They may be getting what they deserve. Punishment and persecution are not the same. Peter wrote that a Christian should not suffer as a murderer, as a thief, as any kind of criminal, or even as a meddler (1 Peter 4:15). Punishment is what just people give to those who are evil. Persecution is what evil people give to those who are good.

Persecution did not seem to be an option for the first Christians. It was part of the job description. Take Jesus Himself as a case in point. If anyone lived in submission to the Father, it was He. If anyone displayed mercy and goodness, it was our Lord. Yet the historical records indicate that Christ's enemies schemed about how they could murder Him after He had performed miracles. Ultimately, the best man history ever saw was put on a Roman execution rack by religious and political authorities.

Are good people really persecuted? Maybe Christ, the disciples, the early Christians. But those were different times, weren't they? After all, Nero was not one's average ruler; his lions had a strange diet. The whole Roman world overdid its cruelty. People had to get used to a new religion. Couldn't the first few hundred years after Christ have been an historical fluke? Of course, thousands died for Christ, but that was so long ago.

If we live according to the Beatitudes, we will be persecuted. It still goes on today. Church historians estimate that more Christian men and women have died for their faith in the twentieth century than in any other comparable period in history. People have died in Uganda, in China, and in Russia. We had a Romanian woman on our seminary campus who, before she arrived, was hounded by the communists and forced to flee with nothing from her homeland. Her husband was murdered. She is a beatitude kind of person who wanted nothing more than to bring other Romanians to faith in Christ. That is still her passion. From 1981 to 1985, the Peruvian government or rebels martyred thirty-five thousand Christians. Christian leaders in Central America have told me about three hundred pastors who were tortured and murdered for their faith in Jesus Christ.

If we live a beatitude kind of life, will we be persecuted? Will we be reviled? Will people speak falsely against us? In the comfort of the United States, we may think we are exempt, but I know of people who have lost their jobs in major corporations because they refused to bend on what they believed right.

Why do people attack those who are living righteously? One reason is, they are different. They march to the beat of a different drummer. They have a different set of standards. And in a world that prizes conformity, difference is often looked upon as dangerous. Some people cannot tolerate those with different values and worldviews. What is more, beatitude people become a kind of conscience in a community. It bothers those who have no integrity to live and work with people who play by the rules. What's-in-it-for-me people are put off by what-can-I-do-for-you people.

The reasons for persecution may be numerous, but Jesus said, "Blessed are those who are persecuted because of righteousness." A couple of times in my life I have been reviled and lied about. At first I was somewhat overwhelmed to discover what I thought was good, others considered evil; to find what I thought was mercy, others found objectionable; and to learn what I knew was right, others viewed as grounds for job dismissal. I went to God and filed a complaint, "Lord, they are on my back; Lord, they are persecuting me." Now I expected that the Lord would say, "My, how I pity you. I want you to know how terrible I feel about all of this." Instead God said, "Congratulations!"

What kind of nonsense is it when the Bible tells us to rejoice and be glad about persecution? If we are feeling the pain of rejection and persecution, God's reply of "Great!" seems like a callous put down. Yet He is not being flip; we should rejoice for two reasons.

We should rejoice if we suffer because of righteousness. We are in great company; the prophets took their licks, too.

Ever notice how people we admire, who are now dead, may have been reviled and persecuted when they were alive? I remember Martin Luther King. We now name streets after him and a holiday has been set aside in his honor. Yet throughout his life he was cursed and he was ultimately martyred. The greatest president of the United States, Abraham Lincoln, was a man who was mocked, scoffed at, and ultimately assassinated. He is a hero now, but he was not in the 1860s.

When we look at the prophets of the Old Testament, men who stand out above all the crowd, who receive our acclaim and our admiration, we find they were persecuted and despised while they lived. In fact, Jesus said to the people of His day, "You build tombs for the prophets, and it was your forefathers who killed them" (Luke 11:47). If we live according to righteousness, if we live for God, we are in great company— that of the prophets and the thousands that followed them.

During the Watergate scandal, President Nixon had an enemies list. People in Washington who found that they were on that list were highly complimented. It was an honor to know that the President hated you. Our enemies, not our friends, are a true test of who we are. If we walk a different path, some will speak evil of us. When that happens, we are in good company. Those who have stood above the crowd have been characterized by one thing—evil people scheme against them.

We can rejoice not only because we are in great company but also because we have a great reward. Jesus said our reward would be great in heaven. If anyone but Jesus had said this, we might think it an exaggeration. If we suffer for His sake, we will receive a significant bonus.

Sometimes the idea of rewards bothers people. At least one altruistic soul says, "I am righteous for the sake of righteousness; I don't want to live for rewards." What we must recognize, though, is the difference between rewards and incentives. Incentives have nothing to do with the act; but rewards, at least as the Bible uses them, are always the product of the act.

In one of Charles Schultz's *Peanuts* comic strips, Schroeder is playing the piano and announces to Lucy that he is learning all of Beethoven's sonatas. Lucy, leaning on the piano, says, "If you learn to play them all, what will you win?" Schroeder is upset and says, "I won't win anything." Lucy walks away and says, "What's the use of learning the sonatas if you don't win a prize?" Lucy was turned on by incentives.

My wife, a piano teacher, once tried to teach our children how to play. We gave them quarters for practicing. My son and daughter were mercenary, so they practiced. Unfortunately, quarters were all they got out of their piano studies. Giving quarters was an incentive, but it wasn't a reward. No relationship existed between the quarters and the piano playing.

The reward of practicing is playing the Beethoven sonata. A man is mercenary if he marries a woman for her money because money is not the proper reward for love. But if a man marries the woman he loves, that's the reward. It's a proper connection.

What do we get if we suffer because of righteousness? The answer is Him. As we live the beatitude life, we enter into an eternal relationship with God. We may not understand all that means, but Jesus tells us it is great. To really have God because God has us, is to have an eternity in which we are the objects of His grace, mercy, and special love. When we come into a relationship with God, whatever that involves, we can only describe it by the word *great.*

Some things are certain. When we go through the waters, they will not overwhelm us. When we go through the fires, they will not wipe us out. In the midst of the persecution, He is with us. If we are compassionate and blameless peacemakers, we should not be surprised if some people sing dirges rather than anthems. Even if we are sometimes persecuted, He didn't oversell the job. Good company. Great benefits.

ELEVEN

MARKET
DEFENSE

Edward C. Bentley, the mystery writer, began his novel *Trent's Last Case* with an intriguing question. He asked, "Between that which matters and that which seems to matter, how will the world know that we have judged wisely?" That, it seems, is a foundational question of life. How do we judge between what matters and what seems to matter? To inhabitants of the marketplace, business matters. They get up very early and go to bed very late, and they give up what is valuable in order to build the bottom line. And yet few men come to the close of life, lie on a deathbed, and wish they had spent more time at the office. What matters and what seems to matter is often hard to distinguish.

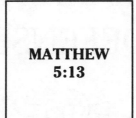

MATTHEW
5:13

To others what matters is power. They spend the money made in business to gain a position of power. Perhaps it's a seat in the House or Senate; or if they are multimillionaires, they run for president of the United States. What matters they think takes place in Washington, London, or Moscow. But many people who have served in political life realize eventually that power really didn't matter much at all. After all, when all is said and done in the capitals of the world, infinitely more is said than done. And even those in power cannot control much of what happens.

How will the world know that we have judged wisely between what matters and what seems to matter? Jesus' disciples never asked the question, but He gave them a surprising answer anyway. He told them they mattered, but He said it in a curious way: "You are the salt of the earth" (Matthew 5:13).

The young carpenter/preacher, not much older than thirty, spoke those words to His disciples. Most of them were evidently His same age or perhaps a little younger. They had yet to make their mark in business; they had not established a sphere of influence; they were not political leaders; they were not born of nobility. They were ordinarily ordinary; some were fishermen, others probably farmers, and one was a tax collector. None of them was particularly religious. And yet to those mostly uneducated men, some speaking with country accents, Jesus said, "You are the salt of the earth." And his "you" was emphatic.

In the ancient world salt was highly valued. The Greeks believed that it contained something almost divine. The Romans sometimes paid soldiers with salt. If a soldier did not carry out his duties, others said he was not worth his salt. And the association of value with salt is still with us. Even today if we know someone who embodies genuine quality or goodness, we say, "She is the salt of the earth."

The ancient world valued salt for several reasons. But the question is, which of those reasons did Jesus have in mind when He said, "You are the salt of the earth"?

Salt was valued as a seasoning agent. We say "Pass the salt," because we recognize that salt has a way of bringing out the flavor in food. Even long ago Job asked, "Can flavorless food be eaten without salt?" (6:6). So perhaps Jesus meant that His disciples were to bring a flavor to life, a zest to living.

In like manner, we should season life. In a world with an overriding sense of futility, we should bring joy. Even though we are people who mourn, we also know the grace of God. That ought to bring holy laughter. Unfortunately, that has not always been true of the citizens of heaven.

Some time ago, a public relations firm in New York conducted a study of what outsiders thought about the church. The unchurched respondents had three major negative reactions. First, the church always asked for money; next, it was always sad; and finally, it always talked about death. That kind of salt doesn't have much flavor.

If Jesus was talking about the flavor-giving qualities of salt, He was saying to His disciples that they mattered in this world because only they made life palatable.

People in the first century also understood salt as a symbol of purity, perhaps because salt was glistening white. As far back into antiquity as we can go, the earliest pagans offered salt to the gods. And Leviticus says that an offering to God must be accompanied by salt; if there was no salt, the offering was not acceptable (2:13). So when Jesus said we are the salt of the earth, perhaps He was saying that we are of value because we can display pure motives before a decadent culture.

In a culture that has perfected the art of lying, we ought to be known for our honesty. When we give our word, people should be able to count on it. In a world in which a thousand billboards proclaim the excitement of sexual looseness, our lives should stand for sexual and moral purity. Perhaps that's what Jesus had in mind.

Salt also creates thirst. Even today Arabs take salt to force them to drink liquids and avoid the dehydration caused by the desert. Salt forces them to drink before they sense the need. If that's the case, then Jesus was saying that we are of worth because we cause people to thirst after God.

But Jesus probably had another quality of salt in mind— its ability to preserve. Farmers and fishermen who heard Jesus speak those words would have thought of the way they used salt most often—to preserve fish and other meat.

After catching fish in the Lake of Galilee, the fishermen sold them in the capital city of Jerusalem, many miles to the south. Transportation was slow and refrigeration nonexistent, so they would salt down the catch. When a farmer killed a cow, he would salt the meat, the only method of preservation.

In many parts of the Bible, the righteous are seen as a force that preserves a decaying society filled with the germs of its own disintegration. Christians are worth their salt because they keep that decay from spreading as rapidly as it might.

Paul described in Romans 1 what happens in a society that has no preserving influence; it is eventually destroyed. Paul could have been reading tomorrow morning's newspaper. What was unthinkable in our culture thirty years ago is now promoted as something right and wonderful. In such a world Christians are important because they can partially stop the rot.

The city of Sodom was synonymous with evil in the ancient world. Located near the Dead Sea, it was evidently a city of commerce, where people came and went, bought and sold, boasted and rotted all at the same time. If we had gone to the Chamber of Commerce and asked them what they really needed, they might have said a convention bureau to attract people and more money to the city. If we had gone to the city fathers and argued for a campaign to bring in permanent residents who were upright and honest, they probably would have treated us like a bad cold. They might have argued that such people don't spend money as fast as the convention crowd.

In the biblical story, we're told that if just ten righteous people could have been found in Sodom, the city would have been delivered. Unfortunately, they couldn't be found and the destruction of Sodom was inevitable.

The French culture of the early 1700s was in the process of decay. The king had a motto: "After me the deluge." He was absolutely right; that was a prophetic voice. The deluge came and France was ripped apart by the French Revolution.

Just twenty miles across the channel, the English culture had the same rot. Historians have described at length the moral corruption of English culture. And yet England did not go through a revolution. What spared it? Its mighty navy? Its suave diplomats? Its politicians? Its police force? No. The country was spared, as historian and president Woodrow Wilson insisted, because in 1703 a man called John Wesley was born in England.

In Wesley's early years his heart was strangely warmed, and he became a citizen of the kingdom of God. He reached out and won others to Christ, and the historians believe that it was in large part the righteous Methodist movement, spread like salt throughout the land, that delivered England from a revolution.

The safety of a nation does not reside in its military genius, its armies, or even its atomic weapons; it comes from the character of its people. Throughout history, civilizations have fallen like decaying trees. The outward push may have come from an enemy, but the country fell because of inward rot.

We are significant if we are beatitude people, meek and pure peacemakers, though sometimes persecuted. We are like salt in a decaying society.

But Jesus implied that we should be aware of two things if we are going to be salt in the world. First, we must be in touch with our culture. One thing about salt is that it must come into contact with meat. If we leave it packaged, it does absolutely nothing.

Throughout history, religious types have often taken the salt out of society. With the monastic movement, monks with good motives withdrew from society to live holy lives separated from the evil of the culture. That was never, however, the biblical example. Jesus sent His disciples forth as sheep among wolves; a wolf pack is the most dangerous place in the world for sheep. We are to be in the world, but not of it. Both of these are commands.

Whenever the church becomes a salt warehouse, it has missed Jesus' basic lesson that salt must come in contact with meat. If we don't relate to non-Christians in their culture, we won't make much difference in society.

Second, we must retain our distinctiveness, that is, our saltiness. From chemistry we know that salt is sodium chloride, and sodium chloride as we know it cannot lose its saltiness. So what was Jesus talking about?

In ancient times two kinds of salt existed. One salt was relatively pure, but another was impure. The relatively pure salt was made through the evaporation of clean sea water. But most of the salt in Palestine was taken from the Dead Sea, which was filled with white minerals that resembled salt. Farmers piled the impure salt behind their houses and used it for fertilizing their fields because a small amount of salt benefited some soils. But when the rains came and pounded on that mound of salt, often the true salt, the sodium chloride, would be washed away. A useless, white sandy substance was left. Farmers couldn't even throw it out on their fields because it had a hardening effect on the soil. Instead they would throw it out in front of the house when they wanted a hard path, and men would walk on it.

If salt loses its distinctiveness, it is worthless. And that's true of those of us who are citizens of the kingdom and are called to be salt in society. If we lose our unique Christian qualities and become like society, we make no impact. We become the problem instead of the solution.

As Christians we matter because by being part of society and having the grace of God displayed in our lives, we preserve that society from evil. But we must come in contact with society and be distinct from it in order to make a difference. If we really belong to Him and are beatitude people, we are salt to the society.

How shall the world know that we have judged wisely between what matters in the world and what seems to matter? We must first accept Jesus' judgment that we matter to Him. On the basis of that, we can decide wisely how to spend our lives. In pouring out our lives like salt, we will find our true value.

Jesus didn't call us to be sugar; He called us to be salt. Salt irritates sometimes, but it also preserves. He called us to make a difference. And to do that is significant. The world will know we have chosen wisely when the real values of life are revealed.

Between what matters and what seems to matter, we should know what counts because we count to God.

TWELVE

MARKET
OFFENSE

The sun is the light of the world. But at night, when the sun is busy brightening the other side of the earth, the moon becomes the light of the world. The moon, of course, is only reflected light. Whatever light it has comes from the sun. In much the same way, Christians are the light of the earth. While Christ is away, we reflect His light. In John 9:5, Jesus said to a dark world that He was its light. But in the Sermon on the Mount He says that we are the light of the world. Just after calling His disciples the salt of the earth, Jesus said, "You are the light of the world." The contrast is interesting.

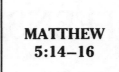

MATTHEW
5:14–16

Salt is negative in that it keeps something bad from happening—it keeps food from decaying. Light is positive in that it causes something good to happen—it enables us to find our way in the dark. And Jesus said we are the light of the world. In some ways that's one of the highest compliments ever paid to the people of God.

Jesus was not saying that we will make a difference by sheer will power, but by being related to Him. He went on to make two points about light. First, you can't miss it. He expressed this by saying that a city set upon a hill cannot be hidden. Hill cities in the Holy Land were impressive sites. They were built there because it was cool; the sea breezes acted like air conditioning in an arid land. And they were built on hills because the location helped them to defend themselves against invaders. Fighting was a lot tougher going uphill than downhill. The mark of Palestinian cities is that they are always in view. At night they glow in the distance.

When we are the light of the world, everyone will know it.

We cannot reflect His light and remain obscure. We cannot hide His light. God doesn't call us into the secret service. Either secrecy will destroy the discipleship or the discipleship will destroy the secrecy. We cannot live light-filled lives in our society without standing out, without having people notice us. They may not like us, and they may persecute us; but they will know we are there.

Second, you use light to help people see. If we buy a new lamp, we don't cover it up; we put it where it will give light to everyone who enters the room. The lamp Jesus spoke of was probably made of clay with oil and a wick in it. A lamp being difficult to light and relight, people put it under a noncombustible measuring bushel of porous clay but only for safety and reduction of light when they went out or to bed. Otherwise they used a lamp for light because that was its purpose.

When speaking of salt, Jesus implied the culture was rotting. When speaking of light, He implied the world was covered with moral and spiritual darkness. The only way for people to see clearly what matters is for us to become light. In so doing we bring a moral and spiritual influence that enables people to see what is there, and to find their way to God.

Jesus said, "Let your light shine before men, that they may see your good deeds and praise your Father in heaven." Jesus did not say that someone will see our good deeds and admit what outstanding, marvelous people we are. God's light does not shine in our external righteousness; it displays itself when we live with an awareness of our need of God's grace. Out of our sense of need comes a merciful and peace-loving spirit. Like light, we simply shine.

When Stephen was being stoned, the record in the book of Acts declares that his face shone like that of angels. I doubt that Stephen ever attended a face-shining seminar. I'm confident that Stephen didn't even know that his face shone. People who live in the light are not conscious of their own light. People who only reflect light do not brag about how bright they are. There are no 1,000-watt beatitude people. People living in the Beatitudes are more conscious of their own darkness, of His grace, and of His light than they are of how much light they reflect. But they do shine, and groping people who see them find their way to God.

Whether we are in business, politics, or some other life pursuit, what really matters is that we be light. And it is imperative that the light shines in the darkness.

Over the years I've had many friends say to me, "I'm in an office where there is not another Christian, and it's rough. The things that go on there are disgusting. I wish I could get out of it." I understand the tension. Our natural tendency is to withdraw under such circumstances. We like to draw as little attention as possible to our distinctive values. If someone gives us a "God Is Love" lapel pin, we wear it under our suit coat where no one will see it. That way we won't get any hassle. We know we should let our light shine, but we're concerned about being misunderstood.

But God needs our light where the world is the darkest. The blacker the night the greater the need for a light bulb. If the bulb does not shine, it's not because of the darkness. Darkness cannot put out a light. If the darkness increases until it is as black as a cave, it is still not dark enough to extinguish a light. No one yet has smothered a light by increasing the darkness. Darkness gets darker because the light fails. When we fail to reflect Christ's light, we let the darkness win.

Jesus did not call us to be magnificent chandeliers for people to admire. He called us to be a single bulb in a back hall to keep people from breaking their necks when they go to the bathroom in the middle of the night. He called us to make a difference in the darkness. Doing so makes us significant.

On June 5, 1910, American short-story writer O. Henry spoke his last words: "Turn up the lights—I don't want to go home in the dark."

As lights in the world, our mission is to make sure no one ever does.

THIRTEEN

FULFILLMENT RATE

In one of his poems, Robert Browning asked the question, "Why with old truth needs new truth disagree?" It is a good question and one that implies that human beings often expect new ideas to replace old ones rather than enrich them. The people of Christ's day might have expected that Jesus would discard Old Testament truths. Matthew pictured Christ as a Healer of the sick and a Preacher of good news (4:23). This young carpenter had suddenly burst upon the scene and captured people's imaginations. People flocked to Him from every part of Israel. They wanted to hear what He had to say. When Jesus pro-

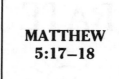

MATTHEW 5:17–18

claimed the good news of the kingdom, people understood the words *good news* in a specific way. The original word translated into these two words was used by the Greeks to announce a victory. Because they believed that all victories came from the gods, good news meant a divine announcement of peace and happiness for the Greek nation. The Romans took the word and used it to speak of anything that had to do with the emperor. If a herald announced an emperor's birth, his enthronement, one of his decrees, or some battle he had won, the proclamation was called good news.

When Jesus announced the good news of the kingdom, the people recognized a declaration normally associated with the gods or a king. He enforced His announcement by healing the sick; and, as a result, He won the hearts of many people. These people must have wondered what was going to happen to the old system if Jesus planned to set up something new. If He erected a new kingdom, would He dismantle the old?

During the French Revolution, Robespierre and his confederates decided that the only way to establish something new was to tear down the old. They completely changed the calendar, renaming years, months, and days of the week. They even changed from a seven-day week to a ten-day week. They renamed the streets and boulevards of Paris. In all of this, they tried to destroy France's past in order to establish something new.

In the 1960s a number of young radicals in the United States argued that the old ways built-up over two hundred years had to go if justice and equality were ever to be established. They wanted to lay new bricks instead of repairing the mortar on the old.

When Jesus heralded the kingdom, the people must have wondered what He would do with the Law and the Prophets. Would He turn His back on it? Of course, the conservatives were concerned that the past be kept; the radicals perhaps would like to have had the past removed. What was Christ's view? What did He mean by "Do not think that I have come to abolish the Law or the Prophets; I have not come to abolish them but to fulfill them" (Matthew 5:17).

Jesus declared these words about not abolishing the past with authority. The phrase "I have come" connoted authority and was a way Jesus often referred to Himself. He was reflecting who He was—the One who existed before the creation of the world, the One who knew His birthplace and when and where He was to die. As one old country man said, "If I knew where I was to die, I'd stay away from the place." Jesus, knowing where He was to die, set His face toward Jerusalem. Israel referred to the Messiah as "the Coming One" (Matthew 11:3). In using the phrase "I have come," Jesus identified Himself as both Messiah and God.

Jesus also demonstrated His authority by the phrase "I tell you" (Matthew 5:18, 20, 22, 28, 32, 34, 39, 44). To the people of the first century who were used to listening to the rabbis speak, the phrase was something new. When the rabbis spoke, they gained their authority from the past. They would refer to the Old Testament laws, the traditions built on those laws, or to some previous rabbi's teaching. No record exists of any rabbi in all of Jewish history speaking out of his own authority.

With the phrases "I have come" and "I tell you," Jesus authoritatively spoke about not abolishing the Law and the Prophets. But He didn't use just phrases. He gave two lessons—one in astronomy, the other in penmanship.

Jesus said that the Old Testament would be around as long as the universe, that is, "until heaven and earth disappear" (Matthew 5:18). Its Law and its Prophets will not be discarded like some old relic. Jesus was saying that the Old Testament and its teachings have His authority behind them, and they will continue until time is ended.

We may think that the Old Testament was some ancient book for Jews and not for Christians, yet the Old Testament was the Bible of the early church. When they met to worship, they had only the Old Testament. We can't understand the New Testament without the Old, and Christ's full authority is behind the Old Testament. If we claim to be a citizen of the kingdom, if we pledge our allegiance to Jesus Christ, then we must give allegiance to the book that He honored.

After peering through a telescope at heaven and earth, Christ examined the written Law with a microscope. He said that "not the smallest letter, not the least stroke of a pen will by any means disappear from the Law until everything is accomplished" (Matthew 5:18). The smallest letter in the Hebrew alphabet was about the size of an apostrophe. The least stroke of a pen would be a small line that distinguished Hebrew letters. It would be like the top and bottom lines on

the capital *I* that distinguish it from a lowercase *l.* Christ's
lesson about letters was His emphatic way of saying that all
of the Law and all of its teachings will continue.

Christ put His full authority behind the Old Testament
with His words and examples, but what did He mean by "not
abolishing the Law"? Some elements seem to have been
abolished. God gave Israel a whole menu of foods that they
could not eat. They could not eat pork, rabbit, shrimp, or eel.
Yet according to Mark, Jesus declared all foods clean by
saying "nothing outside a man can make him 'unclean'"
(7:14–19).

Whole chapters of Leviticus are devoted to telling people
how to sacrifice animals and grains to God. Very specific,
very detailed. Today most of us do not feel we should make a
trip to Jerusalem and offer a sacrifice. Even if we did, the
Jewish altar and temple do not exist. Why did Jesus talk
about not doing away with the Law? What about many of the
other regulations of the Old Testament? Many of them we do
not and cannot follow today.

Some find the answer to Christ's denial of abolishment by
dividing the Law into three parts—civil, ceremonial, and
moral. The first two had to do with Israel's government and
religion, and the last with the Ten Commandments. In this
view Christ was referring only to the Commandments. Because Israel was no longer under the direct supervision of
God, the civil laws didn't apply. The ceremonial laws about
sacrifices would no longer be binding after Christ's death.
The moral law of God existed in the Old Testament and
would be repeated in the New Testament, so Christ did not
come to abolish the moral law. This view seems satisfactory
initially, but it is not without problems.

Why do the Old and New Testaments never make the
distinction between the three types of law? The Law was

simply given and God's people were to obey it. God never said, in effect, obeying traffic lights and attending church were less important than not killing someone. The whole force of God's righteousness seemed to be behind all three types of law. After all, Jesus was very specific. He talked about minute pen marks not disappearing, and He seemed to be including not only all the Law but all the Prophets. The phrase "Law and Prophets" was a way of denoting the whole Old Testament.

The interpretation of Christ's words must revolve around the meaning of *fulfill* (Matthew 5:17). If we understand the word as meaning "to fill full," then what Christ was saying becomes clearer. The Law and Prophets were pencil sketches, and Jesus Christ was the painting. All of the details of those pencil sketches would be fulfilled in that painting. The painting filled those sketches full.

In Matthew 11:13, Jesus declared, "For all the Prophets and the Law prophesied until John." What did the Law and Prophets do until the time of John the Baptist? The Law and Prophets anticipated Christ.

How did Christ specifically fulfill the Law and Prophets? Christ directly fulfilled many Old Testament prophecies. Micah 5:2 said Christ would be born in Bethlehem, and that was where He was born. Christ also indirectly fulfilled a number of prophecies. In Matthew 2:15, Christ's parents fled to Egypt to escape Herod. When they later left Egypt, Matthew explained that this was a fulfillment of Hosea 11:1, "Out of Egypt I called my son." Hosea was writing about Israel that had left Egypt for the Promised Land, but the broad outlines of Israel's history pointed forward to Christ. One example was Israel's forty years in the wilderness. Moses told Israel that God tested them to show "that man does not live on bread alone but on every word that comes from the mouth of the LORD" (Deuteronomy 8:2–3). Christ spent forty days in the desert; and when Satan tempted Him, He quoted Moses' words (Matthew 4:4). So the experience of Israel pointed to Christ's experience.

The relationship of the Old Testament to Christ is like the link between the details in Leonardo da Vinci's *Last Supper* and Christ. Christ is the central figure in the painting, but subtle touches also draw the viewer's attention to Christ. The beams in the ceiling all focus on Him; the hands of the disciples point toward Him. Some Old Testament writers directly described Christ's life; others used "beams and hands."

Perhaps the event that filled the Old Testament more full than any other was Christ's death. The Law prescribed a whole system of sacrifices to deal with sin. For fifteen hundred years, day after day, week after week, and especially year after year, the people brought their sacrifices. These offerings signified that sin brings punishment and only death and blood could release someone from that punishment. Those thousands of dead animals pointed forward to a sacrifice. That's why John the Baptist exclaimed, "Look, the Lamb of God, who takes away the sin of the world" (John 1:29).

Such events from Christ's life as His birth, temptation, and crucifixion give full meaning to the Old Testament, but He also filled full the Law and Prophets with His words. In the last part of Matthew 5, Christ took the laws about murder, adultery, divorce, oaths, retribution, and neighborly love and enriched their meaning. These laws were like empty jars, and He filled them full. He showed that the laws were not dealing with just external standards but also internal values.

Whether we study the furnishings of the temple, probe the messianic passages in the Psalms, or delve into the details of Isaiah 53, we see Christ. Just as the fetus is fulfilled in the adult human, so the Law and the Prophets are fulfilled in Christ's works and words. He is the fulfillment of the Old Testament.

In the ancient world craftsmen often fitted together stones of different colors to make a picture, or mosaic. One of the earliest mosaics is the "Standard of Ur," which is dated about 2500 B.C. In this mosaic the artisan used pink sandstone and lapis lazuli, which is blue stone. He cemented stones on both sides of a two-foot piece of wood. On one side he pictured an army going to battle; on the other, using the same materials, he depicted a king or noble. These two mosaics on one piece of wood were used like a banner or flag; the decorated wood was an emblem of the kingdom of Ur. If a person saw only the side with soldiers, he or she had a distorted view. The kingdom had soldiers, but it also had a leader. When we read the Old Testament, we may see only endless details; but when we take those details and arrange them properly, we see the King.

FOURTEEN

JOB
EVALUATION

"If any man seeks for greatness," wrote Horace Mann, "let him forget greatness and ask for truth, and he will find both." Even if we agree that seeking after truth is a worthy journey, we must still answer the question, "What is truth?" Christ identified some of His truth with the words *these commands,* for He said, "Whoever practices and teaches these commands will be called great in the kingdom of heaven" (Matthew 5:19). In contrast, He warned, "Anyone who breaks one of the least of these commandments will be called least in the kingdom of heaven" (v. 19). What commands did Christ

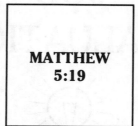

MATTHEW 5:19

have in mind? The Pharisees might have thought He was referring to the Law and Prophets; they had been doing their best to keep the commands of the Old Testament. Unfortunately, they were seeking greatness rather than truth, and their observances of Old Testament commandments were shallow and external.

Christ came not to abolish the Law and Prophets, but He wanted to supply a complete understanding of them. Therefore, the words *these commands* must refer to more than just Old Testament revelation; they must include Christ's interpretation of it. It was only through a true understanding of the Old Testament that the hearers of Christ's sermon could surpass the righteousness of the Pharisees. The Pharisees were actually least in God's kingdom because they were violating the spirit of His commands. Although the commands have the backdrop of the Old Testament, they are best understood as the commands of the Sermon on the Mount.

Christ had challenged His listeners to be salt and light. In the last part of Matthew 5, Christ gave a number of commands in explaining the true spirit of various laws. In essence, He was saying in the Sermon on the Mount, "I am the fulfillment of the Old Testament; and now as a King establishing a kingdom predicted in the past, I am giving commands. Your standing in the kingdom will depend on your obeying and teaching these commands."

Despite what Christ said about the relationship between our keeping His commands and our standing in the kingdom, we are tempted to minimize His commands. We want the truth on our side, but we don't always want to side with the truth. We may feel this way for two reasons. One is that we don't keep the spirit of the Law, so we avoid our responsibility by concluding that Christ didn't really mean what He said. Christ will teach about murder, adultery, and divorce in the last part of Matthew 5; and like the Pharisees, we will initially applaud His words. But when He gets to the heart of the matter, we will not like what He has to say about anger, lust, and selfishness. We'll rationalize that. He really didn't mean that anger was the source of murder, and that anger as far as God is concerned has the same penalty as murder. We get angry at that type of teaching and reduce its meaning. That is why Christ warned against breaking the least of the commandments and teaching others to do so. He didn't want us to downplay His words.

Another reason we diminish the importance of Christ's commands is that we are beatitude people trying to show mercy, and we don't know how to balance grace and truth. People who adhere to truth often lack grace; they toss out the truth like hand grenades. And people who promote grace often do so at the expense of truth. So when many of us teach, and I know this tension in myself, we want to teach in a gracious way. Yet in so doing, we sometimes minimize Christ's commands.

Chapter Fourteen

I know how difficult it is to teach on divorce when some of my listeners are divorced people. Divorce is painful enough, and I don't want to cause more pain. I find myself wanting to sidestep the truth. I want to be gracious; I don't want to be severe. But Jesus keeps saying, "If you are going to represent Me, you must interpret My truth correctly." And in what manner I interpret that truth will determine whether grace and truth kiss each other.

If I were a physician, I know it would be difficult to tell someone that he had terminal cancer. I wouldn't want to do that; I'd rather tell him that he had a hacking cough or his suspicious lumps were benign. But if I know he has cancer and I try to understate that, I have not been faithful to him as a physician. Misrepresenting the truth about cancer can destroy him.

"Truth without charity," wrote Josua Swartz, the seventeenth-century German clergyman, "is often intolerant and even persecuting, as charity without truth is weak in concession and untrustworthy in judgment. But charity, loyal to truth and rejoicing in it, has the wisdom of the serpent with the harmlessness of the dove."

When we are beatitude people, bankrupt of spirit, mourning over sin, and in submission to Him, we will hunger after righteousness. He will fill us; and out of His mercy toward us will flow mercy to others. As we receive mercy, greater will grow our longing to be pure. In the process of becoming pure, we will truly see God who is all truth. As His truth becomes our truth, we will share that truth with grace because we genuinely know the God of both truth and grace. That gracious imparting of truth to others will make us great in His kingdom. But the whole process of knowing and sharing truth starts with God. As Matthew Henry noted, "Nothing can make a man truly great but . . . partaking of God's holiness."

Democritus, the Greek philosopher, pictured truth as lying on the bottom of a clear pool of water. Some people see it immediately; others position themselves to see their own reflection. Pharisees followed the letter of the Law because it mirrored themselves. Beatitude people see below the surface of truth. They understand the spirit of His commands, and they practice and teach them.

What we do with God's truth is all important. In His kingdom, it will determine whether we are creatures great or small.

FIFTEEN
WORK RULES

To teach my son mathematics, I might begin with addition. I'd start with easy figures: 7 plus 5 is 12, and 5 more is 17. After we get that column added, my son might say, "That's it; I guess I've got it." "No, there's more to it," I say. "We will have to go to some larger numbers." So we add 225 and 325 and 621. "That's 1,161," my son exclaims. "No, that comes to 1,171," I patiently state. "You forgot to carry the 1 from the first column." "Well look, it's just 1," he complains. "No, it's 10," I counter. "If we're dealing with 1,000, what's give or take 10?" "If we're talking about your allowance, ten is a lot; it's five weeks worth. If we're talking about miles, it will take you several hours to walk it."

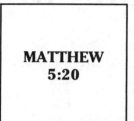

MATTHEW 5:20

"You are picky, picky, picky," he says. "I'm better at it than my sister; she'd miss it by 30."

"It doesn't matter that you're better than your sister. You've got to get it right."

"Whenever I come across 225 and 325 and 621, I'll remember that it's 1,171," he jokes.

"Sorry. That won't do; it isn't just getting the bottom line correct. You've got to do it intuitively. You've got to learn the process, not just the result."

"Look, you're really discouraging me; I don't think I have the ability to add up a column of figures. Why do you have to insist on the right answer?"

"That's just the way it is with arithmetic. I can't change it. I'll work with you. I'll help you. I'll try to get you to understand how it works. But you've got to get the correct answer."

What happens in learning mathematics also happens in learning to pitch a baseball. If I am completely ignorant about baseball and want to learn to pitch, I may get a knowledge-able friend and go out to a ball field. The friend shows me how to grip the ball to throw a fastball or curve. Then he takes me to the pitcher's mound. He says, "You see that white thing about sixty feet away; that's home plate. When you throw the ball, you've got to get it over home plate."

And so I wind up and throw the ball. My first pitch goes wild to the left. My friend throws the ball back. The next pitch goes to the right, but it's only half a foot off. And I say, "Getting closer!"

And he says, "You're getting closer, but you've got to get it over the plate."

I throw five more pitches, and they all miss. I laugh. "Widen the plate a bit. Maybe double it."

"No, you can't double the plate. You've got to get it over as it is."

"Look," I reply, "I'm not sure I can do that. What does it matter? If we had a nice wide plate, I could get it over."

"Sorry, that's the way the game is. I can't make the plate wider. I can give you some more pointers, but you've got to get it over the plate."

"Boy, you're really being arbitrary, aren't you? Insisting that I get it over the plate."

"No, it's not arbitrary. If you miss the plate four times in a row, the batter goes to first base. I don't care how well you throw fast balls or curve balls. If you don't get it over the plate, you can't be a pitcher."

"Why couldn't you ease up and suit the game to my ability?"

"No, you've got to suit your ability to the game. I can work with you, but I can't change the standard."

In the mathematics and baseball illustrations, we see the problems of a teacher working with a student. Jesus was a master teacher, and He wanted to get across to the people of His day what it took to be righteous. He said, "For I tell you that unless your righteousness surpasses that of the Pharisees and the teachers of the law, you will certainly not enter the kingdom of heaven" (Matthew 5:20).

Jesus had to explain "righteousness" to two different groups. One group was the Pharisees. They knew how to throw fast balls and curve balls, and they could add a column. They didn't always get throwing or adding right, but they got them right more often than other people did. Therefore, they were looked at as the standard of righteousness of their day. Jesus wanted to show them that no matter how righteous they were, they were short of the righteousness required to enter the kingdom of heaven.

He was also talking to His disciples. He said that how they responded to God's commands would determine their place in the kingdom. The disciples were to hunger and thirst after righteousness. Christ wanted them to know what righteousness was.

The Sermon on the Mount offers an interesting combination of goals and grace. The Pharisees understood the goal, or thought they did. If all we have is the goal, we do one of two things with it, especially when the goal is righteousness.

First, we will fudge it. It's righteousness give or take ten, fifteen, or fifty. Or we make home plate two-feet wide. Second, we will become dismayed. Goals by themselves can throw us for a loop, discourage us, make us feel bankrupt. That's not bad if it makes us recognize that we still don't understand arithmetic and motivates us to ask for more help. If we go back to our friend and ask him to watch the way we throw, that's a good sign. Unfulfilled goals can drive us back to grace. And grace is somebody coming alongside and giving us the ability we don't have on our own.

If, on the other hand, we have all grace and no goals, we don't ever get any place. We don't understand what is required of us and what grace should do in our lives.

We can't fudge goals we don't have. We can't give ourselves credit for getting close. We can't make up the goals in arithmetic to match our ability. Or even our feelings. We can't urge an umpire to take the motives of the pitcher into consideration. We can't ask the umpire to be less strict on the rookie than on the veteran. We can't do that; if we fudge, we destroy the standard.

In the Sermon on the Mount, Jesus has been talking about the characteristics of the people who inherit His kingdom. He said they were folks who were bankrupt in spirit. They mourn over their inability to be righteous and that causes them to be meek, to be dependent on God. They hunger and thirst for a righteousness they don't have. And out of that hungering, grace comes, and God fills them. Such people are merciful; they become pure in heart; they become peacemakers. Jesus went on to say that these people stand in such contrast to society that they are like salt on decaying meat. They are like a well-lit city on a hill at midnight. We can't miss them.

Jesus' preaching led the people to wonder if these were revolutionary thoughts. Was Jesus bringing in a new standard? Was He doing away with the Law and the Prophets they had followed for seventeen hundred years? Jesus said, "No, I want you to know that I am related to the Law and Prophets in such a way that all it taught is fulfilled in me."

The history of the Old Testament led to the history of Christ's life. The ceremonies pointed to Him. The animals offered on the altar pointed to Him. The food laws pointed to Him. The Old Testament was the pencil sketch, and He was the portrait. He fulfilled it. He also fulfilled the Law in that He filled it full of meaning. For the Pharisees, those jolly good fellows who thought they could be righteous on their own, He wanted them to know that the standard was greater than anything they realized in the Law. For the disciples, who would hunger and thirst after righteousness, He wanted them to know what kind of righteousness to seek.

The people of Christ's day, like most in our day, thought they could keep the Law by simply keeping its letter. We can't blame them for that. That is the way law operates in a society. When I pay my income tax, the tax collector doesn't give a rip about whether or not I do it with good feeling. He doesn't care if I am a patriot or if I am loyal to the president. My motives don't matter. All that matters is that if I owe seventeen hundred dollars I pay seventeen hundred dollars. If I do, he's off my back for a year. I don't have to check a square that says "I'm a patriot."

A wife may decide on a given day to murder her husband. She may feel like doing it, but the law will never bring the case to court. She may think about it; she may wish that she had the opportunity. But until she takes the axe to him, the law can't go after her. A man may want to rape a woman. He may play with that in his mind, fantasize about what it would be like, but he'll never go to jail for thinking about rape. It's only when he commits the act that he goes to prison. The district attorney cannot make a case on what a person thinks about.

The people of Christ's day, like those in our day, didn't get convicted for their motives, so their main concern was the letter of the law. But God was concerned with the heart of the matter, and what matters is the heart.

When Grover Cleveland neared the end of his life, he lamented, "I have tried so hard to do the right." We may sometimes share Cleveland's thoughts; but as we think about what Jesus had to say about righteousness, we have to conclude that we will never be able to add up the figures or get the ball over the plate. But if we sense that bankruptcy, we are in good shape. Jesus said, "Blessed are the poor in spirit, for theirs is the kingdom of God." We can settle matters with God through Jesus Christ.

The law should drive us back to grace; the goals should drive us back to God. And knowing the goals, we see our need of grace; and understanding grace, we discover what it means to hunger and thirst for the kind of righteousness that God gives those who trust Him. That righteousness is not just conforming our behavior to the letter, but conforming our hearts to the Spirit.

SIXTEEN

OUT OF CONTROL

"A reservoir of rage exists in each person, waiting to burst out," wrote Dr. R. J. Beaber of UCLA. "We fantasize about killing or humiliating our boss or the guy who took our parking space. It is only by growing up in a civilized society of law that we learn the idea of proportionate response."

In the Sermon on the Mount, Christ demonstrated that the proportionate response of the law may cover up the purposeful rage of the heart. He said our righteousness must exceed that of the Pharisees who pass muster in their society by keeping the letter of the Law. Instead their hearts are evil.

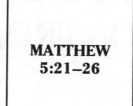

MATTHEW
5:21–26

Jesus represented six illustrations to show what the Law of the Old Testament was really about. The rest of Matthew 5 gives those illustrations. If we're going to understand the illustrations, however, we must be aware of at least four things.

First, we must read them in context. We will miss what Jesus was driving at if we look only at individual paragraphs or sentences in the Sermon on the Mount.

Second, we must keep in mind that Jesus preached in Palestine, and Near Eastern preachers and teachers loved to tell stories. They were their stock-in-trade. What is a bit frustrating is that they often told stories without explaining them. Jesus' parables are stories, but they don't work in the same way we use illustrations. We turn to illustrations to explain something abstract. The Near Eastern speaker just tells stories and allows the listeners to figure out the point for themselves. The listener comes to the lesson intuitively.

Third, not only are the stories unexplained, they sometimes contain radical statements. Jesus said we have to hate our family before we can be His disciple (Luke 14:26). That's strong stuff. But He was not saying we must cherish animosity toward those closest and dearest to us; He was establishing the point that our devotion to Him will make our relationship to our family seem like hate. The contrast is hyperbole.

Finally, Jesus wanted to pound home the principle that the law was not simply the letter; it was the spirit. An individual keeps the law in the heart; outward conformity has little to do with true law keeping. If we don't understand that principle, we simply turn the Sermon on the Mount into another set of laws.

The first of the six illustrations that Jesus gave about the Law came from the sixth commandment—"Do not murder." That was a safe place to begin because the Pharisees, the disciples, and most of the crowd could say, "I've never killed anyone, so I'm comfortable with that. That's good." It's always comfortable to have the preacher talk about other people.

So Jesus began by saying, "You have heard that it was said to the people long ago, do not murder, and anyone who murders will be subject to the judgment" (Matthew 5:21). The listeners didn't have printed Old Testaments, much less New Testaments, so Scripture was always read to them. In the synagogues the Law was divided into seven sections, and seven different men stood up and read parts of it. Then somebody else read a passage from the Prophets, and finally another person got up and interpreted it. So Jesus spoke about what they had heard—"Do not murder. Anyone who murders will be subject to judgment."

Actually the Ten Commandments did not talk about judgment, but the Jewish teachers combined Numbers 35:30–31 with the commandment. The Numbers passage prescribed the conviction process and the punishment. In adding consequences to the commandment, the teachers changed its emphasis from a moral law to a civil offense. They focused on the punishment rather than on the deed.

Jesus continued His teaching about murder with an illustration. He said if the Jewish teachers concentrated on the legal side of murder, that is, on the judgment about it by magistrates, they should also legislate that anger be dealt with in the local courts. Anger as the motive for murder deserves its day in court.

The word Christ used for anger was the one for slow meditative anger, the anger we nurse to keep it alive. It was the kind of anger that plots to get even, to get back. It is like P. G. Wodehouse's character who "spoke with a good deal of animation about skinning you with a blunt knife."

Anger lies at the heart of murder, and Jesus argued that it ought to be dealt with if teachers were going to talk about civil courts. The motive leads to the deed. And then He said, "Anyone who says to his brother, Raca, is answerable to the Sanhedrin," the supreme court of that day. The term *raca* was an Aramaic word, which might be translated in English as "blockhead," "stupid," or "idiot." He was not talking about a word spoken in jest but a hate-filled put-down, a denigration, the expression of anger and perhaps murderous intent.

He said, "Anyone who says, 'You fool!' will be in danger of the fire of hell." To call someone a fool, or dull thinker, was not some easy-come, easy-go slang slinging; it was a way of saying a person lived as if there were no God, a morally and spiritually corrupt person. Using the word *raca* was an attack on a person's mental ability, but using *fool* assaulted on a person's moral integrity.

If a murderer deserves to go to hell, then the fire-breathers and the mudslingers merit hell as well. The act of murder may have physical consequences and in that sense be worse than the thought of murder; but as far as God is concerned, the latter groups are as guilty as a murderer who beats someone to death. God deals with motives; He knows whether or not we have righteousness on the inside.

Somebody may want to get off the hook by arguing that Jesus Himself got angry. That is true. One time He was furious about the Pharisee's legalism (Mark 3:5). The religious leaders were incensed that Jesus had healed a man on the Sabbath, and Jesus became deeply upset at them because their stupid religion kept them from realizing that good was being done. Later on, He called the Pharisees hypocrites and fools (Matthew 13:13–33). That was a statement of fact. They were morally bankrupt. He was making a judicial judgment. When Jesus was angry, it was because of injustice and sin; His anger was not a personal attack. At times anger can be the fruit of righteousness. For example, dope peddlers should make us angry. We should be furious at pornographers who pervert God's good gift of sex or those who unjustly treat those who cannot fight back.

Jesus was not talking about anger that leads to reform, but that which ends up in murder. We usually get angry at personal affronts—"You insulted me, and I want that made right. You understand!"

When Jesus was falsely arrested, taken to a kangaroo court, spit upon by the soldiers, crowned with thorns, mocked by the people, and nailed to a cross, He didn't say a word. When He was reviled, He did not revile again. When He hung on the cross He said from parched lips, "Father, forgive them, for they do not know what they are doing" (Luke 23:34). So anger against injustice is not the same as anger against petty slights. The crucifixion was not a petty slight, but Jesus treated it that way. If He could do that with hell-invented torture, how much more should we with minor tensions.

Anger against injustice sometimes gets perverted. It starts out as anger for a cause, and then it becomes a personal thing—like blowing up an abortion clinic. We can be against abortion without being against abortioners. If our righteousness degenerates into personal anger, we come under the judgment of God's law. That law deals with the spirit as well as the letter. We keep God's law not merely by outward conformity, but from the heart. And since that's true, Jesus said we need to do everything we can, as quickly as we can, to make matters right when anger destroys relationships. He used two illustrations to get this across.

First, He said that gifts to the church are not as important as reconciliation with a friend. We often try to cover up an offense in one place by doing good in another. Embezzlers may put an extra offering in the collection plate. Jesus said that church going will not cloak a ruptured relationship with a friend. Offering God a gift does not camouflage a wrong.

If we have something against a friend and she doesn't know about it, we can settle that before God. But if we both know about it, we must make it right. Then we can come back and offer a gift. Putting money in the collection plate, going to church, singing hymns, reading the Bible, and having devotions doesn't cover up a fractured relationship with another person. That must be settled before sacrificial service. That's what righteousness is—dealing with what we know is wrong.

Reconciliation is important because if the hostile feelings and thoughts I have toward a brother are left unresolved, I cannot worship God. As the psalmist put it, "If I had cherished sin in my heart, the Lord would not have listened" (Psalm 66:18). It is better to leave church early and keep God waiting, and then come back, than to think we can conceal a ruptured relationship with religious exercise.

I've been in congregations where people refused to talk to one another. They sang hymns, prayed, and gave money, but they despised people who worshiped with them in the church. God doesn't give us good marks for our external conformity. When we know something is wrong, if we are really interested in righteousness, we must settle these disputes with others.

Christ's second illustration takes the matter of reconciliation a step further. We are to settle conflicts not only before we go to church but also before we end up in court.

In the Greco-Roman world, the law allowed for citizens' arrest. If someone picked another's pocket, he or she was guilty of breaking and entering. If a person stole clothes from the public bath, a common crime, or a slave from another person, any citizen could arrest the thief and drag him or her into court without calling the police. At the court the judge would pass sentence and turn the criminal over to the jailer. The convicted thief would be taken to what we would call a debtors' prison. Robbers were kept in this prison until they reimbursed the victim for the goods stolen. But prison was a tough place to make money. Jesus said that a person should work out a settlement before a judge gets involved. He was stressing the urgency of rectifying a squabble.

If a matter is not handled quickly, anger can become open hostility, and problems left to fester will only get worse. More important, if we died with unsettled contentions, what would it be like to stand before a God of love and holiness?

Chapter Sixteen

Thus for practical and theological reasons, controversies should be settled immediately.

Dame Sybil Thorndike, the British Shakespearean actress, was married for many years to the distinguished actor Sir Lewis Casson. After his death, she was asked if she had ever thought of divorce. She replied, "Never. But murder often!"

Keeping the sixth commandment is more than not committing the act of murder. God is interested in our motives. He never lets us get away with murder. He knows our mind.

SEVENTEEN

COMPOUND
INTEREST

One young college student perhaps spoke for many in our generation when he said, "Look, just because some old man spent a night on a mountain and came down and said, 'You shall not commit adultery,' why should I let that spoil my fun?" When Hugh Hefner first published *Playboy* magazine in the 1950s, it was a national scandal. Times have changed; the magazine no longer seems very risque. It has become nearly as acceptable in our society as *Time* or *Newsweek*. Hugh Hefner's Playboy Clubs in the United States have all shut down because the "bunnies" seem tame as rabbits. Hefner's spun out his

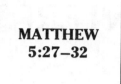

MATTHEW
5:27–32

philosophy that all sex is just good, clean fun. People should be able to enjoy it with anyone they please, at any time they please, anywhere they please. Anyone objecting to this philosophy received the dreaded label "puritan," someone who lived to take the joy out of life. Adultery isn't wrong; it's merely a puritan hang-up.

Even more striking is that Hefner's philosophy of unrestrained hedonism has a great many adherents in the academic and religious worlds. Ethics teachers argue adultery is not wrong as long as it is done by consenting adults and nobody gets hurt. Under these circumstances, sexual looseness is nobody's business and certainly not something to alarm us.

Worse yet, some religious people try to baptize Hefner's free-wheeling philosophy into the Christian faith. They maintain that Jesus came to teach us to love, and as long as two people really love each other, whether married or single, whether in an illicit affair or a proper affair, love covers everything. After all, isn't love really the religion of Jesus?

These religious leaders not only advocate a destructive philosophy but are trying to get Jesus to approve acts that He would not have endorsed at all.

In *The Merchant of Venice,* Shakespeare put it this way:

> In religion,
> What damned error, some sober brow
> Will bless it and approve it with a text,
> Hiding the grossness with fair ornament?

In the Sermon on the Mount Jesus addressed the sins of our age, and He talked about adultery. As a Near Eastern preacher, Jesus set the points of His teachings in sharp contrast to each other, with no middle ground.

Jesus was developing an argument, and we must see the argument in its context. In the Sermon on the Mount He was calling people to a relationship with Him that will affect their relationship with others.

The adultery passage cannot be understood apart from the preceding verses. Jesus began His Sermon by saying that those who sense a poverty in spirit, a mourning over their sin, and a deep dependence on God will hunger and thirst for righteousness. God will fill them with righteousness, and they will show it in a merciful attitude, a pure heart, and a desire to make peace. Even though they may be persecuted, they will be salt and light in a putrified and dark world. Their hunger for righteousness must exceed that of the Pharisees, and it will if they understand that God provides internal rather than external righteousness.

To prove His point about God's filling, Christ gave six cases to demonstrate the priority of the internal over the external, or relationships over rules. The first case was murder and anger, and He showed that the motive for murder condemns us as much as the act. If murder is a capital crime, then anger and its offspring name-calling, which leads to murder, ought to have their day in court, too. To put it in another way, if we cure anger, murder won't be a problem. Christ used two stories to illustrate why it is important to deal with anger. His gift-giving and court-threatening stories show that repairing relationships is both essential and urgent. Anger is the symptom of a broken relationship, but the outgrowth of our inward righteousness should be positive relationships.

Christ's second case was about adultery and lust. Here again, He showed that the hungerer's righteousness is superior to the Pharisee's righteousness because it is driven by the spirit rather than the letter of the law. The hungerer's righteousness starts in the heart; it focuses on relationships rather than on rules.

As long as the religious leaders had never met a woman at some Mediterranean motel, they could heartily agree with Christ's repeating of the seventh commandment, "Do not commit adultery." But Christ didn't stop at adultery. He said, "Anyone who looks at a woman lustfully has already committed adultery with her in the heart" (Matthew 5:28). Adultery is not just an act; it has to do with the heart. When Jesus talked about looking at a woman lustfully, He was not simply talking about sexual desire. That was given to us by God and is portrayed in the Bible as a good gift. Admittedly the gift is often labeled "Handle with care," but sexual desire comes from God.

By the word *lust,* Jesus did not refer to sexual desire or the normal attraction between men and women. The word *lust* is the same word in Greek that is sometimes translated "coveting." It is desire that focuses on a woman with the view of possessing her or of having an immoral relationship with her. It is a look with a purpose. To put it another way, it is "I would if I could." Only convention, her husband, or the fear of getting caught stops us. The stress of lust is in its purpose. Anyone who purposes in the heart to commit adultery has already committed it in God's eyes.

After Christ's explanation of adultery, He warned that if the right eye or another part of the body causes a person to sin, radical surgery on these parts would be better than to have the whole body thrown into hell. Christ used hyperbole to make His point. Adulterous desires corrupt relationships; therefore, we ought to deal with them drastically.

To interpret Christ's words about mutilation literally can be almost humorous. Suppose I'm having a struggle with lust. I poke out my right eye, but no evidence shows that one-eyed people are less lustful than two-eyed people. I'll chop off my right hand, but no studies verify that one-handed people are less lustful than two-handed people. I could gouge out my left eye, but sexual fantasies will still play on the cinema of my mind. Even if I'm blind, I could go the whole way—amputate both arms and both legs—but torsos are not exempt from lust.

The problem isn't body parts. Jesus used absurdity to show that adultery, like all sin, is serious enough for men and women to end up in hell. We ought to deal drastically with anything that leads us to that. If our magazine reading or our cable TV watching causes us to lust, then we need to cancel our subscriptions. If we find ourselves in compromising positions, we should run as Joseph did from Potiphar's wife.

Lustful desires corrupt relationships. It may destroy the relationship with a friend if a person lusts after the spouse. In general, if a man lusts after a woman, or vice versa, the relationship with the lusted-after person may be shattered whether adultery takes place or not. Because lust is a matter of the heart it should be dealt with drastically and quickly. The impure in heart don't want anything to do with God, and God wants us to have a relationship with Him.

William Byrd, an eighteenth-century Virginia farmer and surveyor, kept a personal diary. He recorded his struggle with lust or, as he called it, the "combustible matter." He kept putting water on the fires, but they continued to spring up. In one entry he wrote: "I neglected to say my prayers, which I should not have done, because I ought to beg pardon for the lust I had for another man's wife. . . . Endeavored to pick up a woman, but could not, thank God."

Thank God, He gives us new desires. We can hunger and thirst after Him.

EIGHTEEN

SEVERANCE AGREEMENT

"You can make divorce as easy to obtain as a dog license, but you can't burn away the sense of shame and waste," wrote A. Alvarez in his book *Life after Marriage*. The Pharisees knew all about licenses, but they knew little about commitment and love. Jesus continued His explanation of the letter and spirit of the law by citing a third case. Having lectured on murder and anger, adultery and lust, He then addressed divorce and selfishness. In Deuteronomy 24:1–5, Moses explained the divorce law. In essence, a man with a proper certificate could divorce a woman if he found something indecent about her,

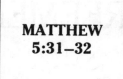

MATTHEW
5:31–32

but he could not remarry her if she was divorced by a second husband. Because women were treated like property in the ancient world, Moses gave the law requiring a divorce certificate as protection for women. A woman was regarded as no different from a saddle. If a man tired of his wife, he could simply dismiss her. To guard her rights, Moses set forth three principles in the law. First, a man could only divorce a woman for a serious cause. The word *indecent* in Deuteronomy 24:1 is used of human defecation; so Moses was referring to something filthy or vile—a serious matter.

Second, the man must give the woman a written certificate of divorce. Rabbis indicated that this certificate must be given before two witnesses so they could examine whether a man's accusations were serious. A written bill of divorcement gave a potential second husband a guarantee that he could legally marry a divorced woman. Without this, blood wars could develop between the first husband and a second suitor.

Third, a man could not take back a twice-divorced wife. Marriage was not a revolving door that allowed a man to leave his wife and take her again. Marriage is too sacred for that. So Moses gave his divorce law not to loosen divorce restrictions but to tighten them. He was not saying anything goes. In teaching that divorce must be taken seriously, legally transacted, and not trivialized, Moses was actually moving back to the original design of marriage.

By New Testament times the focus of Deuteronomy 24 had changed from protecting a woman to finding all the possible grounds for divorcing her. That is where legalism leads—to the letter of the law. The rabbis concentrated on one word: *indecent.* Since it was broad, they had a field day with it. One rabbi interpreted it as meaning loss of attractiveness. In this case, a man could divorce his wife if he no longer felt warm toward her. Rabbi Hillel and his followers said *indecent* could refer to a woman burning a man's dinner or speaking disrespectfully of him. Other rabbi schools took a narrower view and limited the meaning to some moral indiscretion, such as a woman tempting a man by letting down her hair or uncovering her arms or legs, both considered indecent in the first century.

When people follow the letter of the law, they are always looking for loopholes. Jesus came into all of this garbage of the first century and declared that no mercy or purity existed in outward conformity. A man could follow the law exactly yet show his wife no mercy and cause her to live an impure or adulterous life. To understand the spirit of the law, we must comprehend God's original design for marriage. Christ didn't elaborate about this in Matthew 5, but He did in Matthew 19.

In Matthew 19, the Pharisees asked Jesus, "Is it lawful for a man to divorce his wife for any and every reason?" (v. 3).

This was a trick question. If Jesus answered no, He went against the rabbis because they thought some reasons existed for divorce. If He replied yes, He went against all the rabbis because not all rabbis thought every reason was valid.

Jesus answered their question by going to Genesis 2 instead of Deuteronomy 24. He said that marriage was an act of God, not a legal contract or even a union of mutual love. Society did not invent marriage, they received it. Marriage was not only an act of God, but also a union of a man and woman. Marriage was not like a business partnership, which might easily break up when times get rough. It was like the union of the head and torso; it was a dynamic, integral relationship. As the bow and the violin are one instrument. As the lock and the key are one unit. As the hand and the arm are parts of a single body. Therefore, we cannot break it. That was God's original design. That's what God intended. That's what is involved in the Genesis statement.

The Pharisees avoided what Jesus was saying about the creation and union of marriage. They wanted to talk about Deuteronomy 24, so they asked, "Why then . . . did Moses command that a man give his wife a certificate of divorce and send her away?" Moses never commanded anything; the Pharisees had upped the ante. Moses had simply provided protection for women who were treated as property, but the Pharisees implied that a man had no choice. They weren't concerned about relationships; they were caught up in legalisms.

Jesus answered their second question, but not in the way they expected. Moses gave the law because of men's hard hearts, not because God approved of divorce. In the oppressive ancient world, God was showing His mercy to women. Divorce was not in God's original design; His standard was one man with one woman for life. Only fornication, that is, sexual looseness, can break the bond between two people. If a man and woman are in a one-flesh relationship, sex with someone else by either spouse breaks the union and God's ideal. But if sex outside marriage is not involved and a man sends his wife away, he commits adultery in marrying again, and he forces his first wife to commit adultery. Several people will be forced into relationships outside the will of God. Adultery then takes on all kinds of forms. To avoid the multiplying of adulteries is to practice the spirit of the law; it is to understand Christ's teaching about man's hardness of heart and God's original design for marriage.

Christ was asserting that at the heart of marriage stands commitment, not love. In the Bible marriage is for the tough-minded. The disciples responded to this emphasis on commitment by throwing up their hands, "If this is the situation between a husband and wife, it is better not to marry" (Matthew 19:10). At least the disciples recognized that dogged attention to the relationship is the heart of marriage. Marriage is not for as long as love shall last; it is as long as life shall last. It is a promise given and a promise received. Running out of romance provides no reason for running out of a marriage.

The very first divorce in the world must have broken God's heart; unfortunately, it did not have the same effect on man. Men have now been casting these commitments aside for thousands of years. In recent times, women have joined the freedom march. The results of divorce have been devastating. As Jo Coudert observed in *Advice from a Failure,* "The divorced person is like a man with a black patch over one eye. He looks rather dashing but the fact is that he has been through a maiming experience."

Divorce is a serious matter. As someone else said, "It is the psychological equivalent of a triple coronary by-pass." It is not about pens but scalpels, not about ink on a page but incisions on a heart. What concerns God the most centers on the heart. Although divorce destroys God's original intention for marriage, it is not the unpardonable sin. When we sense an impoverishment of spirit, a feeling of guilt, we ought to hunger after God's grace and forgiveness. We may not be able to restore the marriage bond, but we can renew our union with Him.

NINETEEN

PROMISSORY NOTE

I attended a religious university in the South that had a lot of rules; and as part of admission, every student agreed to abide by them. The school had a rule against card playing. They said playing cards was sinful, but they really were against the deck of cards used for poker or bridge. Using those cards was wrong because they were associated with gambling and wasting time; so if students used them on campus, the school authorities would expel them. But the students could play Rook. Even though the game is similar to bridge it was allowed because it used different cards I had a roommate who almost flunked out of school be-

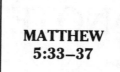

cause he played so much Rook. But if he had ever played bridge, he would have been kicked out of college.

The morality, or righteousness, of the behavior at that university had to do with external values, not internal. It had to do with keeping rules. A student could in effect take an oath not to play cards, but as long as he didn't deal aces, kings, or queens, he kept the rule. Using cards with other pictures on them didn't matter even though playing those card games could have caused him to flunk out of school. That's what happens when righteousness becomes only a system of rule keeping. We make distinctions so that we can do one thing and not the other. Whether or not you believe card playing is a moral issue is not the point. If you believe it is, you destroy the spirit of the card-playing rule with devious interpretations of it.

In the Sermon on the Mount, Jesus wanted us to understand that God is not primarily concerned with right behavior, but with a change of heart and right attitudes. The righteousness of which He spoke does not come through rule keeping.

The righteousness of God requires a complete change of viewpoint, a complete change on the inside. That's why He began with what we call the Beatitudes. He began by saying blessed, or approved, are those who are destitute in spirit, for theirs is the kingdom of heaven. Just as we might say "Good appetite promotes good health," Jesus was saying "A great sense of inner need promotes righteousness." But we can't leave it there. People with good appetites starve to death.

But if we turn to God to meet our need, to satisfy our hunger and thirst for righteousness, we will be filled. We are not filled with a new set of rules to follow nor a bunch of religious regulations, but with mercy. Having received mercy, we become merciful. Concerned now about motives, we become pure of heart; and the pure of heart see God. And out of that purity, we become peacemakers and in that way bear the resemblance of our Father in heaven.

We might think that folks who are merciful, pure of heart, and peacemakers, would always be welcome. But Jesus said that such people are out of step with society. As salt, beatitude people preserve society from decay. As light, they shine in the darkness and lead men and women to God.

All of this emphasizes what is crucial in the Sermon on the Mount. Jesus was not giving us a whole new set of laws. He was not saying, "The Old Testament was tough, but it wasn't tough enough. If we don't get this law-and-order bunch together, we've got problems; so let's make the laws tougher." He was not dealing with laws at all. He was dealing with the inner righteousness that God provides, that catches the mind and heart and makes a difference in life. He was not saying that beatitude people don't keep the rules, but that rule keeping is not their focus. Keeping rules never makes us righteous.

A world of difference exists between behavior that simply keeps a set of rules and righteousness that comes from the inside. Did Jesus point to the most religious people of His day and say, "You've got to do better than that?" No, not quite. He was really saying, "You've got to *be* better than that. You've got to have a completely different kind of righteousness than they have."

The Pharisees thought they could handle righteousness on their own. But Jesus said in the Beatitudes that righteousness begins when we see our need of God. When we feel this bankruptcy of spirit, it will drive us back to Him for the righteousness we don't have on our own.

The kind of righteousness Jesus demands develops from an inward change that God produces. It involves a new starting point, a new beginning, a whole new orientation to life. If we fail to understand that, we fail to understand the New Testament. And people who come to the Sermon on the Mount with this misunderstanding keep trying to make it into a new set of rules. They want to define it so they can keep it.

The Sermon on the Mount is about inner righteousness worked out in life. It doesn't apply to the world nor to the political establishment; it applies to people in whom God has worked. In the last part of Matthew 5, Jesus applied this fulfilling of the law to six areas. Having looked at murder, adultery, and divorce, He came to the fourth area: oaths.

Jesus used this fourth case to again underline the principle that righteousness is not outward conformity to rules and ceremonies, but an inner response of a heart that is merciful and pure and seeks to make peace. He reminded the Pharisees that people had said long ago, "Do not break your oath, but keep the oaths you have made to the Lord" (Matthew 5:33).

No Old Testament passage specifically prohibits oath breaking, but several passages speak about oaths. A person was
not to swear falsely by God's name (Leviticus 19:12) or mis-
use His name (Exodus 20:7). But as a safeguard against frivo-
lous vows, oaths could be taken in God's name (Deuteronomy 10:20). The Old Testament was clear that an oath was a
way to emphasize the truth and importance of what we say.
It set a statement or promise apart in a special way—just as
marriage vows mean that a husband and wife have solemnly
sworn to love, honor, and cherish each other until death
parts them. The purpose of wedding vows is not to keep a
couple from lying to one another. No. Vows sworn to one
another before God demonstrate the importance of what
they are promising one another. It is to say that this is very
significant to us.

winking at best Man -

In Hebrews 6:13–17, the writer recalled God's oath to Abraham. God swore by Himself to make clear that His promise of
blessing to Abraham would extend to future generations.
God took an oath, not because He lies, but to confirm to
Abraham in the most solemn way possible that the promise
He made about land and descendants would be fulfilled. So
when God takes an oath, He's underlining His words, placing
them in italics, putting exclamation points after them. The
purpose of an oath was to show the solemnness and to
reinforce the importance of what was said.

There were two kinds of oaths. An assertive oath said, "I
did it" or "I didn't do it." A promissory oath said, "You can
count on me. I give you my word." In the Old Testament the
oath marked out the most solemn assurances that people
gave to one another. It was used to stress a strong commitment.

By New Testament times, the legalists had focused on the
"name of the Lord" in the oath. God's name, not commitment,

marriage:
Its over when truth breaks down.
Hiding and the coverup — Cat & Mouse game of
client & retreat to concealed.

concerned the religious leaders. And so an oath that was uttered to underline truth, came to undermine truth. They got to the point of saying that the only speech that had to be true was an oath. Then they went a step further. They decided, "But not all oaths matter." Only those that are in God's name, only those in which a person crosses the heart, swears to God, and hopes to die. Those are the ones that really matter. As a result, that whole culture, with its fine tuning of oaths, became a society of liars. Lying under oath became a fine art.

The *Mishna,* a Jewish commentary on the law, had sections on both oaths and vows, explaining both assertive statements and promises for the future, the ones to keep and not to keep. The Pharisees got it down to prepositions. If they swore *toward* Jerusalem, the oath didn't matter. Jesus mocked all of that. In Matthew 23:16–22, He mocked all of their oaths: swearing by the gold of the temple instead of the temple, swearing by the gift on the altar instead of the altar, and swearing by heaven instead of God's throne.

These nitpicking Pharisees were in the same category as people today who reason that bridge is sinful but Rook is okay. Their distinctions are all ridiculous. If anger was the real issue of murder, lust the real issue of adultery, selfishness the real issue of divorce, then deceit is the real issue of oaths. Jesus responded in two ways to the deviousness of the Pharisees.

First, Jesus dealt with it biblically. To the people who said they didn't have to keep their oath as long as they didn't swear by God or by what is sacred, He said, "That's ridiculous, unbiblical, and illogical." If a person is swearing by heaven, earth, or the city of Jerusalem, they are swearing by God. The Old Testament says that heaven is God's throne

(Psalm 123:1), that the earth is His footstool (Isaiah 66:1), and that Jerusalem is the city of the Lord (Isaiah 60:14).

A Pharisee not only swore by geography but also by his head and even his beard. Such oaths didn't matter. God is the Creator of man, so all oaths bring Him in. In other words, we can't get rid of God. Everything we swear by involves God. All of the universe, not just His name, belongs to Him.

The second thing He said was more shocking. Since the Pharisees couldn't leave God out of their oaths, we might expect Jesus to warn them to make sure to keep their oaths. But He didn't. Instead He instructed them not to swear at all. In Matthew 5:37 He told them to let their "yes be yes" and their "no be no." Anything else came from the evil one.

In a world that uses oaths to assure that we speak the truth, we need to have an inward truthfulness that doesn't depend on oaths at all. When we give our yes, it is yes; and when we give our no, it is no. Oath or no oath, when we say something, others can count on it. Men and women who are truthful will be truthful whether they are under oath or not. So we ought not swear in order to say, "Now I am telling the truth."

A society that has a hard time telling the truth signs tightly worded contracts and demands oaths: "Do you swear to tell the whole truth and nothing but the truth, so help you God?" But contracts and oaths cannot guarantee truth. People will lie despite formal agreements or pledges.

Jesus was not talking about rules, about what oaths to take or not to take, about how to frame an oath, about whether we should swear to God or put our hand on the Bible when we testify. If we are truthful people, we don't need oaths to guarantee our truthfulness. Anything beyond a simple yes or no comes because the evil one who controls people encourages deceit.

Because Jesus said not to swear at all, the Quakers believe they ought not take an oath in court, so the government allows them to affirm. They do this out of good motives and for sincere reasons, but affirming something is not much different from taking an oath. This is the same old hair-splitting legalism.

Jesus wasn't against oath taking. He allowed himself to be put under an oath by the high priest (Matthew 26:63–64). Paul put himself under an oath on two separate occasions to emphasize the importance of what he was saying (Galatians 1:20; 2 Corinthians 1:23).

Jesus wasn't addressing whether or not we should take an oath. He was talking about whether or not we are truthful. If we hire high-priced lawyers to build loopholes into our contracts, we are not truthful. When two people have a clear understanding between them, the contract shouldn't matter. In our society we have to sign contracts, and we had better read the small print closely because people write contracts to their own advantage. But not beatitude people. It can't be true of us. When we give our word, that is all we have to give.

We don't tell the truth because we have taken an oath; we tell the truth because we are truthful. Our yes is yes; our no is no. When we begin picking at the loose threads in a contract to go back on our word, we have become like the Pharisees. There is a wickedness to that, and it comes from the evil one. As salt and light, we say, "I know what it says, and I realize that I can get out of it because of the wording, but I gave you my word. You can count on it." Then we are light in darkness. We are salt in a decaying society. We are like God when we keep our word.

Something is desperately wrong in a society when a man guilty of murder gets off because the sergeant put down the wrong date on the warrant. Something is wrong when people get off on technicalities. But we don't rely on technicalities. We rely on truthfulness. We mean what we say. We try to say what we mean. Jesus calls us to integrity. We tell the whole truth and nothing but the truth without oaths and without affirmations. So help us God.

TWENTY

OVERTIME

Ibn Saud, the king of Saudi Arabia from 1932–1953, once had a woman come to him and demand the death of a man who had killed her husband. The man had been picking dates from a palm tree when he accidentally fell, hitting the woman's husband and fatally injuring him. Although the king tried to persuade the woman not to pursue her rights, she insisted on them. Finally, the king said, "It is your right to ask for this man's life, but it is my right to decree how he shall die. You shall take this man with you immediately, and he shall be tied to the foot of a palm tree. Then you yourself shall climb to the top of the tree and cast yourself down upon him from that height. In that way you will take his life as he took your husband's." The woman quickly changed her mind, realizing that in following the letter of the law and demanding her rights, she might lose her right to life.

MATTHEW 5:38–42

In demanding our rights, we often do lose our right to real life, the kind that comes to those who hunger and thirst after righteousness. It is the beatitude life that comes out of a relationship with Him and with this comes a new relationship with other people. It is a relationship that comes out of meekness, mercy, and purity of heart. It is a relationship that seeks to make peace.

When we live that kind of life, we can expect to be persecuted. People will revile us, speak evil against us, and put us down. Our new goal will make us go the opposite way down a one-way street. We'll be bucking the traffic, and that annoys people.

Instead of keeping laws to be righteous, we will have an inward kind of righteousness. Instead of outward conformity to laws, we will have an inner response to the spirit of the law. People who live that way are the salt of the earth and the light of the world. And their light draws others to God. Unless we have that kind of righteousness we have no hope of getting into heaven, because our righteousness must exceed that of the scribes and Pharisees.

Jesus says that His righteousness has nothing to do with rule keeping; it has to do with relationships. And a right relationship with God shows in the way we relate to people.

Like all good preachers, Jesus used examples to drive home His point. He presented six case studies to show that His kind of righteousness has nothing to do with rule keeping.

In the first He centered on the law against murder. He said our concern ought not be whether or not we kill someone—that's where the law starts. Our concern ought to be for relationships—we are to guard relationships and not allow anything to come between us and someone else.

The second had to do with adultery. We can pass laws against adultery, but Jesus said the real problem is lust in our hearts. We ought to deal drastically with anything that corrupts a relationship with another person, with another man's wife or another wife's husband.

Then He talked about divorce. He said we won't solve the problem with stricter divorce laws. They only force people to live together in an armed truce. To solve the problem of divorce, we must go back to God's initial desire for marriage—for a couple to become one flesh, creating a spiritual union as dynamic as the union of the body. When we keep that in focus, the laws about divorce become immaterial. They never even come up.

Then Jesus talked about oaths. He said, "Don't swear," but He didn't say, "Don't take an oath in court." For Christians, oaths should be unnecessary. Our yes means yes, and our no means no. An oath will not make us tell more of the truth. Placing one hand on the Bible and raising the other in a pledge to God will not make us more truthful than when we simply say yes or no. The spirit of truth makes us truthful; taking an oath does not.

In the fifth illustration Jesus dealt with the law of retaliation. "You have heard that it was said, 'Eye for eye, and tooth for tooth'" (Matthew 5:38). The Old Testament repeated that principle of law at least three times: Exodus 21:24; Leviticus 4:20; and Deuteronomy 19:16–21. The Deuteronomy passage is most important for our consideration.

Some say the Old Testament law was savage and blood-thirsty, but that is not true. Actually it was the beginning of mercy. And it is the foundational law of all civilization.

Although it allows retaliation, it limits it by setting restrictions. If a person knocks out my tooth, I get his. And if I poke out his eye, he gets mine. Retaliation as we know it sets out to get more than that. We want to up the ante. But this law limited retaliation. People could only get back what they lost.

In addition to being merciful, the law limited retaliation to the offended. It didn't allow the whole family to get into the act. When wronged, we tend to line up forces of family and friends to retaliate. If a person cuts off my ear, I want to cut off his head. And if I cut off his head, his brother will kill me, and if he kills me, my brother will kill his brother, and pretty soon we have a clan war. The battle between the Hatfields and the McCoys did not start as a family feud. It started with two individuals.

Without the law of retaliation, revenge goes from the individual to the family to the clan to the tribe and ultimately to whole nations. So what seems to some like a blood-hungry law was actually a way of limiting violence and bloodshed.

In the law of the Old Testament, retaliation was not an individual decision, nor was it something one individual could demand from another. It was a principle of justice that was decided by a judge in a court of law.

What is given as a principle of fairness, however, sometimes gets twisted into a law that prescribes vengeance. If a person knocks out my tooth and I know the law, I think I have the right and even the obligation to knock out his tooth.

As it worked out in Israel, the law seldom if ever was applied literally. If I knock out someone's tooth, what good does it do me to get a tooth in return? Both individuals lose a tooth that way. So in court a judge decides that a tooth is worth a thousand bushels of wheat. Or if a person pokes out my eye, the judge may decide that I should be paid four bulls, three cows, two lambs, and next year's crop. The judge tries to determine what a tooth and an eye are worth.

We use this principle in our modern courts. When I seek damages for an injured leg, the court determines the value of my loss and makes the guilty person pay me. But in our culture we have laws that go beyond awarding damages. We make claims for mental pain, inconvenience, and embarrassment. These laws allow more than retaliation. "He took my tooth, so I'm going to get twenty-five times that." When lawyers urge us to contact them if we've been hurt in an accident, they are saying that someone ought to pay for all our grief. So we use the principle of retribution to be vindictive. We're not happy with getting even; we want to get ahead.

When Jesus said, "Do not resist an evil person," He was talking about legal ways to get retribution for what happened to us. We see that in two ways.

First, it is given in relation to the law of retaliation, which is a law of the courts. When Jesus said, "Do not resist the evil person," He meant, "Don't go to court." Don't decide to sue the daylights out of the other person to get your rights. That opposes the law of retaliation. Jesus was referring to Deuteronomy 19:18, which gave people the right to retaliate and to make a false witness pay for what he did to them. He was contradicting it by telling us to give up that right. We are not to retaliate, not to take the evil person to court and apply the law of retaliation. Instead of standing on our rights, we are to deal with others with generosity of spirit, the kind that God has shown us.

To drive home that principle, Jesus gave four illustrations. In the first one, He instructed us to turn the other cheek if someone strikes us on the right one. Approximately ninety percent of the people in the world are right handed. If we punch someone with our right hand, we will hit him on the left cheek. If we try to hit him on the right cheek with our right fist, we won't do anything to him. We can't do anything to him. If I am going to strike his right cheek, I am going to do it with the back of my hand, and in Israel that was an insult. To strike a man on his right cheek, or to give him the back of your hand, was worse than injuring him. The insult was worse than injury. If a man struck a person with the back of his hand instead of punching him in the mouth, he could collect twice the damages. It was considered an affront, a put down. We use similar euphemisms today. The Irish often say, "The back of my hand to you," which means, "You are scum."

If a man reviles us, speaks evil against us, or slaps us on the face, Jesus said not to retaliate. Although we have a right to take him to court, we're not to do it. We're to turn the other cheek.

If he insults us once, he can insult us again. If he makes us feel stupid in front of our friends, we allow him to do it again. We are to give up our rights to retaliate: we are to have a generous spirit.

In John 18:22–23 Jesus followed His own advice. When He stood before the High Priest, someone in the crowd punched Him. Jesus didn't say, "Try the other cheek." He said, "Why did you slap me? If I spoke evil, show me where I spoke evil. If I spoke truth, show me where I spoke truth."

This demonstrates that Jesus was not speaking literally. He was talking about insults, not muggers in the subway. When someone hurls an insult at us, we are to respond in grace.

In the second illustration Jesus spoke about injustice. He said, "If someone wants to sue you and take your tunic, let him have your cloak as well" (Matthew 5:40). The tunic was the undergarment that a man in the Near East wore. It was like a form-fitting body shirt and worn like a long robe. The cloak was like an afghan and worn like an overcoat. The cloak was protected by law. Exodus 22:26–27 decreed that if someone took a man's cloak for security in a business deal, the person had to give it back at night because it was used as a blanket in winter and as a pillow in summer. A fellow needed his cloak at night.

But that was not true of the tunic. It had no such protection. A man's tunic was fair game in a lawsuit. Getting a judgment for a man's cloak was more trouble than it was worth. The winner would spend all his time picking it up every morning and returning it every night. But the tunic was a different matter. People frequently took tunics as security.

But Jesus said to give up rights even to cloaks. Although they're protected by law, we're to give them up to settle a dispute. Our attitude should be, "If you're upset with me and my tunic will make you happy, it's yours. And here's my cloak as well." That's the spirit of generosity.

Our seminary had a business deal with a firm in town that promised to do a job for a certain price. Two things happened. First, they did not do a good job. Second, they charged us almost a thousand dollars more than we had agreed on.

I checked with people in the industry to find out if the firm had any right to do that, and they didn't. So we sent a check for the amount we had agreed on, even though they hadn't done the job well. They responded by billing us for the other thousand dollars. But I knew my rights. I was ready to go to court. I had my case all ready. It wasn't the money, of course, it was the principle. Usually the principle is the money. In this case it was a little of both.

I didn't like being taken advantage of. But the other people on my team advised me to do the generous thing and send the firm the money. They put things in perspective for me by asking, "What if that person, believing he deserves the money, heard you speak? Would he believe anything you said?" So we sent them the check for the other thousand dollars. I gave in and gave up my rights. Interestingly, about nine months later they sent a check to the seminary for close to the same amount we had overpaid them.

In the third illustration Jesus talked about duty and imposition. "If someone forces you to go one mile, go with him two miles" (Matthew 5:41). That too, was a matter of law. When the Persians delivered mail, they made long trips on foot. So mail carriers were allowed to make Persian citizens carry the mail one mile. The Romans liked the idea, so they adopted it. A Roman soldier or official could compel a Roman citizen or inhabitant living under Roman protection to carry his burden one mile.

The word translated *forces* in this passage is used in only one other place. When Jesus fell beneath the load of the cross, the historian said, "They met a man from Cyrene, named Simon, and they forced him to carry the cross" (Matthew 27:32). The Romans had a legal right to make him do it.

The army exercised the privilege frequently. If a soldier got tired of carrying his pack, he could say to a person, "All right, buddy, you carry it." And that person would have to stop what he was doing and carry it. He didn't say, "Let's make an appointment. I'll meet you here tomorrow and carry it then." It was an imposition, but it was a duty. The Jews hated it. And they hated Romans for making them carry their loads.

The Jews held to the letter of the law on this. They measured the mile in steps. One thousand exactly. And they counted every one. When they got to one thousand they stopped, put down the pack, and left the Roman to carry his own load or find another victim.

But then Jesus came along and told them to offer to carry it an extra mile. And to do it with generosity, with a spirit that says "I am not going to count the steps." They were to give up their rights.

In other words, the first mile we do for Caesar, but the second mile, when we do our duty with kindness and generosity, we do for God. And so I say, "I am not going to be held down to just doing my duty. I am not going to chafe under the imposition. I am going to do it with a generous spirit." That is how we are to do our duty, how we are to live as disciples of Christ.

The fourth illustration has to do with requests for help. It deals with what is moral. Jesus said, "Give to the one who asks you, and do not turn away from the one who wants to borrow from you" (Matthew 5:42). This has to do with the law of lending, and it too comes out of the Old Testament. As Deuteronomy 15:7–11 indicates, debts were canceled every seven years. The borrowers loved it. The lenders weren't quite so enthusiastic.

If I were a lender and someone came to me for a loan in the sixth year, I would think twice before giving it to him. If he didn't pay it off quickly, the loan would turn into a gift. The closer the seventh year got, the more tightfisted businessmen became. But Jesus said they were not to allow the seventh year to govern them. Whenever a brother had a need, they were to give generously, openhandedly. After all, these people were not asking for home-improvement loans. They needed money for food.

Jesus wasn't talking about every panhandler who sticks his hand out, and He certainly wasn't talking about lending money for business ventures; they didn't do that kind of thing in the ancient world. He was talking about people in need. Our only consideration should be whether we can help. If so, we are to give generously, without thought of repayment.

In each of these illustrations the overriding principle is that we are not to seek our own rights. When we are insulted, we have the right to retaliate; but we are not to exercise it. If we are treated unjustly, we have a right to our possessions; but we are to give them up. If we are imposed upon, we have a right to set limits, but we are not to insist on that right. When someone has a need, we have a right to our money, but we are not to be tightfisted with it. Instead of being right, we are to be generous.

When we are generous with others, we reflect our Father in heaven. He said, "Let your light so shine that man may see your good works, and in doing so they will see God" (Matthew 5:16). Generosity that doesn't retaliate, doesn't seek what is ours, reflects God. The only people who can live that way are those who know the grace of God. We recognize that in God's grace we don't get what we deserve.

Several years ago, a church I'm familiar with was on the verge of a split. During a business meeting, a man stood up and said, "Look, all I'm asking for is my rights, and I demand my rights."

Another man responded, "If you get your rights, if you get what you deserve, you'll go to hell. Every drop of water this side of hell is the grace of God."

That's the key to understanding the Sermon on the Mount. God has dealt with us in grace, and we are to reflect His grace in all our dealings with others.

TWENTY-ONE

RECONCILED ACCOUNTS

Ramon Narvaez, the nineteenth-century prime minister of Spain, was dying and was asked by a priest, "Does your Excellency forgive all your enemies?" "I do not have to forgive my enemies," replied Narvaez. "I have had them all shot." We often shoot our enemies. To act otherwise is foolhardy; it's better to get them before they get us. Even if we don't fire at them, we rarely treat them kindly. To love an enemy would be an extraordinary feat. That would take a different sort of person with a different kind of righteousness. Jesus said that type of righteousness is internal. It grows out of a relationship with God and into a relationship with other people. It's not legalistic, and it's not something we can define.

MATTHEW
5:43–48

Matthew 5:43–48 is the sixth case in point of this kind of righteousness. "You have heard that it was said, 'Love your neighbor and hate your enemy.' But I tell you: Love your enemies and pray for those who persecute you, that you may be sons of your Father in heaven" (vv. 43–44).

The Old Testament law said we are to love our neighbor (Leviticus 19:18). From the negative perspective it says, "Do not seek revenge or bear a grudge against one of your people." But it adds a positive dimension: "Love your neighbor as yourself." Those who wore their righteousness like a three-piece suit wanted to take a close look at the word *neighbor.* Who exactly did it mean? The person next door? Across the street? Across town? Across the state? Across the country? Across the ocean? Where do we draw the line?

Those folks figured it out. They decided where to draw the line. A neighbor was someone close. To those outside their immediate circle they could be indifferent. And there was a whole mass of people they regarded as enemies and were free to hate. They reasoned that people who weren't their neighbors must be enemies, so they could despise them. In a nice, neat theological way they divided the crowd and almost dignified their hate.

But Jesus said the Old Testament law did not teach that! He said we are to love our enemies and pray for those who persecute us. Other translations add the phrases love your enemy, bless those who curse you, do good to those who hate you, and pray for those who hurt you. The middle two phrases aren't in the best manuscripts, but they are certainly in the spirit of what Jesus was saying. If we are His disciple, if we have a love relationship with Him, we will also love our enemies.

To understand what Jesus meant when He talked about loving our enemies, we need to consider several words in the Greek language translated *love*. One is probably closer to our word *lust,* and is not used in the New Testament. Another refers to the love of friends, and still another to the love of country. But apparently none were strong enough or sturdy enough for the New Testament writers when they talked about God's love for us or our love for others.

The word the New Testament writers used for this divine kind of love is the Greek word *agape.* Outside the New Testament, in classical Greek literature, it is only used five or six times; and it is a weak, anemic word. It could be translated "goodwill." Evidently the biblical writers took this word *agape,* seldom used outside the Bible, and baptized it into the Christian faith, filled it full of new meaning, and gave it strength.

In the New Testament *agape* is used to speak of God's love for us and the kind of love we are to have for others.

One of the characteristics of *agape* love was that it was not primarily a love of the emotions; it was a set of mind, an act of will. It was directed and active benevolence, an attitude that said, "I will do what is best for the other person whether I am dealing with friend or foe."

Immanuel Kant, the philosopher, read these words about loving our enemies and dismissed them as absurd. He insisted it was impossible for people to love their enemies. If we are talking about the feeling kind of love, Kant was right. We can't control our feelings that way. We can't light emotion as we would a match and blow it out as if it were a candle. If we are talking about emotional love, the command is beyond us.

But Jesus was talking about *agape* love, a set of the mind. Putting it another way, I am to deal with every person, whether friend or foe, as if I like them. I seek their highest good, not because I feel like it but because I make it the attitude of my mind. It is directed benevolence. With other loves I feel and then act. With this kind of love I act, and sometimes as a result I feel. Therefore I can love my enemy.

If we wait until we have warm, friendly feelings toward our enemies before we pray for them or act benevolently toward them, we will all die first. But when we act with that person's best interest in mind, regardless of how we feel, we reflect our Father who is in heaven.

Augustine rephrased Jesus' words when he said, "To love those who love you is human; to hate those who love you is demonic; but to love those who hate you is divine." When we love our enemies as well as our friends, we reflect the character of God.

One way to love our enemies is to pray for them. In doing so, we find that it is difficult to go into the presence of God and pray for His will to be done in a person's life and come out bearing anger and hostility toward him. To pray for somebody makes a difference in the way we see and act toward that person. To pray for another person is godlike. To seek the best for our enemy in the presence of God is to discover benevolence toward that person.

We are to bear a family resemblance to our Father in heaven, and one quality that characterizes Him is His indiscriminate benevolence—the way He acts toward His friends and His enemies. God causes His sun to shine on the evil and the good. He sends rain on the righteous and the unrighteous, because it's His nature to do so.

It would be convenient, I guess, to drive through the country and know that fields rich in grain belonged to Christians and that the dry, shriveled crops belonged to non-Christians. But God doesn't work that way. When He sends rain, it falls on believers and blasphemers. When God makes His sun shine, the atheist gets as warm as the Christian. God deals with enemies and friends alike. When we deal with both enemies and friends with their highest good in mind, we are like God.

But God's benevolence and kindness are often misunderstood by unbelievers. God's goodness is designed to lead them to repentance. But many folks misinterpret it as God's indifference toward their sin. If God blesses them with growing grain, a warm body, and a full wallet while they are living in rebellion toward Him, they think God doesn't take their sin very seriously.

An atheist in a small town wrote to the editor of the local paper one fall. "I have conducted an experiment," he wrote. "I have a field by the Baptist church. When the Baptists came to worship, I plowed it. I planted it on a Wednesday night when they were at prayer meeting. And I brought in the harvest while they were having a revival meeting. But I want to report that the field produced as much as any other field I have." The editor printed the letter and added this comment: "What the reader does not understand is that God does not settle his accounts on a Saturday night." Many unbelievers do not understand that. Because they have been blessed, they become indifferent to God; not realizing that in His goodness, He deals with enemies and friends alike.

When He says we are to love our enemies and pray for those who persecute us that we may be the sons of our Father in heaven, He is not urging us to do those things to become God's sons. We do them because we are God's sons. It is a family likeness. We see family likenesses in children's physical appearance and in their behavior patterns. We say of a son, "He's a chip off the old block." Of a daughter we say, "She's the spittin' image of her mother."

When we treat friends and enemies with equal benevolence, when we seek their highest good, we show that we are in God's family.

If we love those who love us, what reward will we get? If we greet only our relatives, how are we different from anyone else? Even the tax collectors do that. The tax collectors were the scum of society in the ancient world. Around April 15th we're not too fond of them either, but in the ancient world they were considered traitors.

Speaking today, Jesus might use the Mafia as His example. One thing that marks the Mafia is that they are good family men. In fact, family is all important to them. They look out for their own, and they wipe out those who threaten them. They love family and kill enemies. If we love only those who love us, how are we different from the tax collectors or a member of the Mafia?

When Jesus spoke of greeting someone, He didn't mean a simple "Hello." To greet someone in the Middle East is to wish the best to them. Their greetings are all bound up in blessing. Blessing on you, blessing on your children, blessing on your children's children. Even the pagans did that. In fact, their greetings were known for that. They were often long and elaborate. If we bless only the people we like, Jesus said we are no different from the pagans.

Jesus was saying that their ceiling ought to be our floor. Their love ends with family and friends, but that should be only the beginning of our love. We start where they stop. The high end of their friendliness scale is the low end of ours.

The reason we do this is to reflect our Father's love to the world. We love our enemies not primarily to make them our friends, but to show them God's love.

Someone once castigated Abraham Lincoln for his benevolent attitude toward southerners, whom the critic considered enemies. Lincoln replied, "What better way to destroy an enemy than to make him a friend." Good response. But that is not why we do it. While it may happen in the process, that is not our motivation. Nor do we do it because we believe that we can draw enough goodness out of their hearts to transform them. That is both simplistic and un-biblical.

The truth is, we can love our enemies and they may spit in our face. They may see our love as weakness and take advantage of us.

We do it to reflect the love of our Father in heaven, who has made us His light in the world. When people see us loving those who do not love us and seeking the best for those who have made themselves our enemies, they see something godlike. And that is the basis of evangelism. Often I have seen people come to faith in Jesus Christ because they saw a Christian who stood out from others, and they wanted to know what made the difference. They heard the melody of the person's life and wanted to learn the lyrics.

The conclusion of it all is found in the last line of Matthew 5: "Be perfect, therefore, as your heavenly Father is perfect." The word used here for perfect does not mean sinlessly perfect. No place in the New Testament does the meaning come close to that. The word was used of a sacrifice offered to God. It had to be perfect, that is, without blemish. It is used and translated most often as *maturity,* as opposed to what is childish. It was used to speak of a teacher as opposed to the student. It's the sense of being well rounded or complete, of fulfilling the function for which it was made. If we say, "That is a perfect tomato for a salad," we are not passing judgment on the character of the tomato. We are speaking of its ability to perform a function, to add flavor and appeal to a salad.

When Willie Mays was reinstated into baseball by the commissioner, a sports writer said of him, "He was probably the perfect ball player." He did not mean that Willie Mays never struck out. Never dropped a fly ball. He meant that Willie Mays was well rounded. He could hit, run, catch, steal, and he knew the strategy of the game.

That was how Jesus used the word *perfect.* We are to be perfect as our heavenly Father is perfect—in the context of love.

Inasmuch as we deal lovingly with people, we are well rounded and complete. As God does not discriminate in showing love, neither do we. We are never more like God than when we act in love toward another human being.

Sometimes as I read this section of the Sermon on the Mount, I feel the poverty of my life. I feel a kind of bankruptcy because this is the kind of person I ought to be and want to be. But I am very conscious that I am not. And that realization drives me back to poverty of spirit, which is the basis of our relationship with God.

The Beatitudes begin by saying "Blessed are the poor in spirit, for theirs is the kingdom of God." This section of the Sermon on the Mount fulfills its purpose if it drives us back to God for the inner righteousness of thought and motive only He can give.

We cannot live this kind of life in our own power. We can't simply decide "From here on out I am going to love my enemies." We may indeed become upright. But our uprightness will be like that of the Pharisees and the teachers of the law. It passes muster with men, but we will never get into heaven with it.

We can only live this life in relationship to God. And in that relationship, God works in us to establish the same kind of relationship with others. A relationship that does not allow us to be satisfied by keeping the letter of the law externally, but gives us an internal desire to keep the spirit of the law.

Alfred Lord Tennyson, in writing about archbishop Thomas Cranmer, said, "To do him a wrong was to beget a kindness from him. For his heart was so rich . . . that if you sowed therein the seeds of hate, they blossomed love."

Like Cranmer, we must understand the heart of God. One enemy is too many.

EPILOGUE

Years ago Joe Bayly, the late *Eternity* magazine columnist, visited some German Christians who had been devoted soldiers in the German army during World War II. Two of them had been put up for promotion to become second lieutenants in the Nazi army. The commandant told them he would approve the promotion on one condition: that they join the Officers' Club. Being a member of the club would require them to attend some wild and rather permissive weekend dances. These young men believed that dancing was wrong because it promoted sexual looseness, and sexual looseness would lead to immorality. Because of their convictions, they turned down the promotion.

Later in their military careers these same men were assigned to the death camps where thousands of Jews were stuffed into ovens and killed. Even though they did not directly participate in the slaughter, they knew what was going on. Yet they never voiced any protest.

When Joe Bayly talked to them many years after the war, they looked back on their experiences with no regret, convinced they had made right decisions. For them, not conforming to social pressure and refusing to dance was an act of righteousness. And conforming to patriotic mass murder and remaining silent while thousands of Jews were burned in ovens left them with no feelings of unrighteousness.

When we set our own standard of external righteousness, we are capable of any evil. When we are filled with His righteousness, no good is too great.

Note to the Reader

The publisher and author invite you to share your response to the message of this book by writing Discovery House Publishers, P.O. Box 3566, Grand Rapids, MI 49501 U.S.A. For information about other Discovery House publications, write to us at the same address.